Maria Gabriela Brito

OUT THERE

Design, Art, Travel, Shopping

Editorial director: Suzanne Slesin
Design: Stafford Cliff
Managing editor: Regan Toews
Production: Dominick J. Santise, Jr.
Assistant editor: Deanna Kawitzky

POINTED LEAF PRESS, LLC.
WWW.POINTEDLEAFPRESS.COM

To Marcio,
for sharing the world with me.

To Daniel and Oliver,
for showing me a world that I
didn't know anything about.

To Carlos and Lizabeth,
for bringing me into this world.

Discov
Design,
and other
Pas

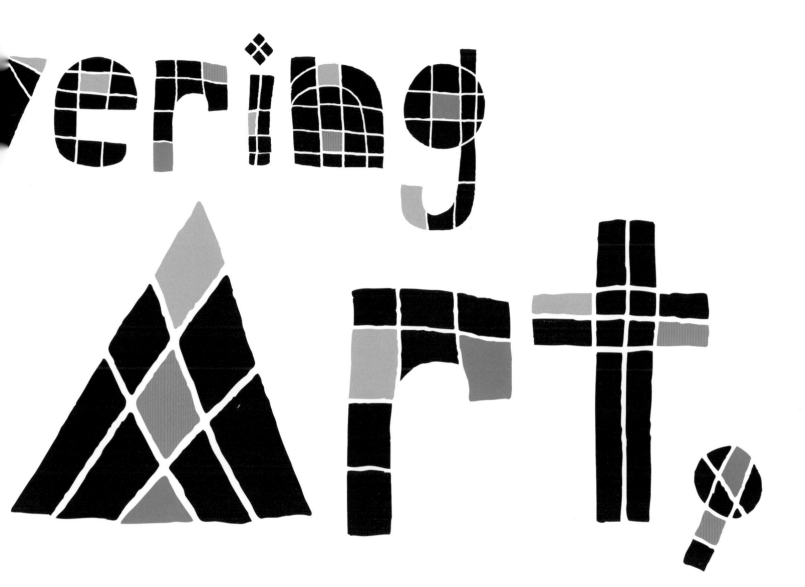

ering Art, sions

MY BEGINNINGS

I was born in Caracas, Venezuela, a very hectic city surrounded by mountains and located about 30 miles from colorful beaches surrounded by palm trees. My parents, Carlos and Lizabeth, although Venezuelan by birth, came from a very mixed background—Spanish, Portuguese, and Corsican blood on my father's side, and Dominican and Lebanese on my mother's. A patchwork of nationalities continues to shape my life today. Being born in the 1970s, I experienced a very interesting and different Caracas from what it is nowadays. Despite the fact that I was pretty young, I still remember my parents, their siblings, and their friends dancing to the disco tunes of Donna Summer and Diana Ross in exquisite gowns and in the most amazing settings. Caracas was known back then as the most glamorous and chic city in South America—full of international celebrities, European royalty, and jetsetters who came to spend weekends partying in Caracas or on one of the paradisiacal Venezuelan islands that are majestically scattered in the clear waters of the Caribbean. The opulence of parties, weddings, birthdays, and any other festive occasion is still very vivid in my mind. People lived to celebrate. I remember always being surrounded by colors, either in my parents' apartment or in my grandparents' house, on the streets, or at the many children's parties, which we called "piñatas," that I attended or that my parents organized for me. Color has inspired my life. All the visual cues I gathered came from the bright blue skies, green mountains everywhere, intense red flowers, interesting people wearing flamboyant outfits, and all the excesses of the 1970s and 1980s. Everywhere I looked, people were dressed in European designer clothes, such as Yves Saint Laurent Moroccan-inspired kaftans, Pucci dresses in the most psychedelic patterns and shades of neon, Fiorucci T-shirts and angel-printed jeans, and Christian Lacroix flamenco-influenced cocktail dresses. Back then, fashion was an imperative among the women of Caracas. It was also a city where I felt I lived in an eternal spring and summer, as the weather was always so agreeable and the sun shone nearly 365 days a year. Colors and details looked even better and more vivid in that light. Many weekends and holidays were spent with my family at the beach, either on the coast in the fabulous archipelago of Los Roques, or on Margarita Island, where my father was born. The colors on these beaches ranged from emerald green to turquoise to ultramarine blue in the deep seas, and the sands varied from pure white to complex hues of terracotta. The trees and plants surrounding the beaches were usually breathtaking, and I was always amazed at the beauty of nature in Venezuela and proud to be a native of such a blessed country. Many years ago, I remember reading *Paula,* a memoir by the famous Chilean writer, Isabel Allende, who lived part of her life in exile in Caracas. She wrote that Venezuela was a country whose soil was so fertile that anywhere you'd throw a seed or the pit of a fruit, ten trees would grow. I couldn't agree with her more. Art

With my dad after seeing *Evita*

With mom on Sixth Avenue, 1983

was also a big part of my life, as my parents and grandparents enjoyed living with it and collecting South American paintings. My maternal grandfather was a medical doctor who would spend weekends with an easel and canvas, recreating the landscapes that surrounded him, or a stilllife that he had purposefully composed for the occasion. We always visited museums. From pre-Columbian to contemporary art, I was immersed in that world very early on. My parents knew many cultural figures, including one of the most amazing kinetic artists of all times, the great Jesús Rafael Soto, whom I fondly remember meeting when I was about six years old. The artistic and cultural movements of the 1970s and 1980s—street graffiti, Pop and Op Art, and color field and photorealism still have a profound impact on my life and my designs. Roy Lichtenstein, Tom Wesselmann, Andy Warhol, Jean-Michel Basquiat, and Keith Haring are the artists that always come to mind when I think about my childhood. My parents loved to travel and always took me on trips to show me the world. But it was a trip to New York in 1983 that changed my life forever. I felt I had always belonged in that maze of streets and skyscrapers, on the subway trains covered with graffiti, and surrounded by the music blasting out of boomboxes in the middle of the street. It was all necessary fuel for my creative life. I saw a Haring drawing depicting two men lifting a radiant heart above their heads, with a barking dog next to them in the subway station on 28th street and Seventh Avenue, and his symbols, which became so distinctive and recognizable over the years, are still imprinted in my early memories of Manhattan. I fell hard and fast for the frenetic pace of people who seemed to represent absolutely every color, ethnic background, and nationality in the world. I knew back then that one day I would make New York my home. Growing up, decorating was also very much a part of my daily life. Latin people love to hang out at friends' houses and live to entertain at home. The whole concept of having a well-put-together house in which to enjoy a good time, surrounded by loved ones, is deeply entrenched in the Latin culture. Lunch, coffee, teatime, Happy Hour cocktails, or dinner were all excuses for people in Caracas to get together at someone's home. Although things have dramatically changed in Venezuela since the time I lived there as a child and teenager, people still want to gather and spend long hours talking, eating, drinking, and watching the busy city from expansive terraces, or in backyards surrounded by green hills. When I was a teenager, my mother asked me to redesign the apartment in which we lived. She said: "Here's the budget; what can you do with it?" So I went and chose all the fabrics with which to reupholster the large sofas and armchairs in the living room. Strangely, although so many years have passed since then, I gave that room a makeover using some of the colors that I'm still drawn to in most in my projects: indigo blue, mustard, and hints of flamenco red. I added vintage wood furniture and a large, contemporary marble-and-glass coffee table. I also reupholstered all the chairs in the large, formal dining room in a blue, red, and mustard striped moiré fabric. In my bedroom, I changed my baby drapes for easygoing white Roman shades, sent old bookcases out to be lacquered in white and cobalt blue, changed all the hardware, and designed a headboard in a patchwork of fabrics. I chose nearly every piece of furniture and also hired the upholsterer, carpenter, and handyman who worked on the project, either through my friends' parents who had used their services before, or with the help of the Yellow Pages and a bit of luck.

OPPOSITE I celebrated my eighth birthday in Caracas, Venezuela, with a strawberry shortcake-themed party, which I planned with the help of my parents. I had decided on a costume party and wanted a sequined outfit.

LANDING IN NEW YORK

Marcio and I in Barcelona in 2011

At the Hole Gallery in New York

Through twists and turns, but mostly via an upward curve, I moved to New York in the very hot and humid summer of 2000. I don't know if it was luck or chance, but after seeing dozens of sterile rental buildings in three days, I was somehow directed to a Venezuelan gentleman. This was the man who was to be my landlord, and, along with his wife, a superb contemporary artist who worked on large-scale sculptures, they were my guardian angels in New York. Her art communicated with me on a much deeper level than any other pieces of art I had ever seen. The apartment was in a stunning landmarked brownstone on West 89th Street, ten feet away from Central Park, and was a nicely sized bright and sunny one-bedroom with high ceilings and all the original details and wood flooring from the early twentieth century. Moreover, the place was furnished with light and charming Scandinavian pieces, and to my absolute delight, it had good art hanging on every wall. I bought a lot of fun vases that I constantly filled with fresh flowers, as well as graphic pillows, Uzbek suzanis, picture frames for family photographs, Tampico Mexican rugs, and a dinnerware set for 12 people, as I knew that I would be entertaining. And entertain I did, from throwing Latin-themed dinner parties to movie and pizza nights, sometimes for four, and sometimes for 20 friends. For many years, I worked in a variety of corporate jobs and law firms after having graduated from Harvard Law School. Although a fabulous experience and an Ivy League dream-come-true diploma, neither being a lawyer nor the intricacies of corporate America gave me any real satisfaction or fulfilled my creativity, which was absolutely bursting inside of me. But living in New York became the most extraordinary experience of my life in and of itself, even when doing the most mundane things in a series of boring jobs, as it passionately fed every cell of my creative soul: The chaotic streets with people always in a rush; the vast number of stylish women who looked as if they had just stepped off a fashion runway; the shop windows all decked out with a clever combination of visual merchandising, marketing, and innovative design; the cultural edge always more at the forefront than in any other city in the world; the galleries, theaters, and museums that showed the latest in art, design, film, and fashion; the restaurants that ranged from molecular deconstructed menus to the simple delights of a Greek diner; and the exciting nightlife that covered every extreme of the spectrum, from glamorous hotel bars like the Bemelmans at the Carlyle to crazy nightclubs like the Limelight, which was built in a place as bizarre as a deconsecrated church. Life operates in mysterious ways. I'm quite certain that extraordinary things happen when one is in the right place at the right time. That is how I met Marcio Souza, my husband, on a boiling summer day in New York. Marcio was born and raised in Rio de Janeiro, an often clashing but magical city, where the beach and the buildings merge together under the watchful eye of Christ the Redeemer, and lush, green mountains surround the city in a sinuous and sensual way. Culturally, Brazil has been known for its amazing soccer teams, bikinis, and supermodels, *caipirinha* cocktails and *bossa nova* music, extravagant carnival parades in February, and a spiritual New Year's Eve party where everyone—and I mean *everyone*—wears head-to-toe white outfits and offers flowers to a female deity called *Iemanjá*, or Queen of the Seas. Brazilians and Venezuelans share many cultural similarities, but when Marcio and I met, we were both busy New Yorkers who were put in front of each other by being in the right place at the right time. Although we didn't start dating right away, we fortuitously ran into each other several months after our first encounter, and it was then that we knew we were meant to be. Eighteen months later, we became husband and wife. Like good New Yorkers, we were obsessed with real estate, and so we decided to buy our first apartment. We really didn't know what we were getting ourselves into! We began our search during a time when the market was quite hot and every offer that we made was considered for only a split second, as we would usually go for properties that would invariably end up in bidding wars. For several months, we visited hundreds of places all over the city and eventually became drained and discouraged. Finally, although it was not in the neighborhood we wanted, we bought a large two-bedroom co-op in Sutton Place. The apartment had lots of character and I saw the potential in its expansive rooms, excellent layout, and high ceilings. I stained the hardwood floors a dark brown and removed the old mirrored walls in the "I love the 1980s" style left by the previous owners. I carefully chose the furniture, including a pair of Art Deco chairs covered in a Senegalese orange fabric that I still own and now display in my current living room. I went to showrooms, thrift shops, yard sales, and antiques shops. My contemporary art collection, which I had started so many years ago, finally found a real home, along with some new pieces chosen by Marcio and me. Two years went by, and I found myself pregnant and wanting to move again. Luckily, Marcio wanted a change too. The real estate bubble had been growing disproportionately and was starting to deflate. We knew that we didn't have much time and that we needed to act quickly. Though a bit unconvinced at first on the telephone, once our real estate agent visited our apartment in person, she was blown away! Despite the fact that our building had two other similar listings that languished on the market, two weeks after we put our apartment up for sale, we got an offer, and two months after that, we closed on the sale and moved to a brand new condominium loft in Chelsea.

OPPOSITE Since 2004, I have collected silver frames from Peru and Mexico to display my favorite family photographs, which I lined up on a console in the Chelsea apartment we now live in. I enjoyed playing with their different shapes and sizes.

MY PATH TO LIFESTYLING®

Although I took several detours, I always knew I wanted to be either a designer, an architect, or an artist. My desire was to incorporate the vast amount of visual information and experiences that I had accumulated throughout my life into my career, and I wanted to do it freely, intuitively mixing and matching the things I loved with the art I loved. Travel, places, people, art, and fashion have all influenced who I am and continue to give shape to my creative process, the process that brings about my designs and the way I perceive the world around me. I was thrilled to recognize that my years of collecting art and the way I had decorated our place had not only accelerated the sale, but had also gotten us the price we wanted. My real estate broker told me about my first apartment: "You would have never sold the place had it not been for the way you decorated it. You have a special eye." Those words stuck in my mind, and after my son Daniel was born in 2008, I intuitively felt I was ready to start my business. I took a chance and bet on my talents to mix and match furniture from different styles and periods with fabrics, colors, wallpaper, and contemporary art. When I checked my address book, I had more than 600 names of contacts in the art world. I knew I could make people happy and channel their passions and interests through interior design, decorating, and art. I also knew that people in New York were too busy to do it themselves, that there were major misconceptions about collecting art, and that many people wanted to learn about contemporary art but were afraid and intimidated by galleries, auction houses, and even visiting art fairs. I was on to something. As soon as I was settled in New York, I wanted to start my own art collection, motivated by my past and the enormous opportunities that the city presented. I craved good art, and going to galleries, museums, and art fairs became my weekend pastimes. One day, I stopped by my former landlord's apartment, and his lovely wife welcomed me and invited me to see her studio. Since we shared many things in common, including our colorful cultural background and citizenship, she knew I would enjoy the impromptu visit. She unveiled a rather large bronze sculpture of a woman sitting on a stool repairing the ripped pieces of a Venezuelan flag. She called it *Reconciliation*.

She did not have to say a word or explain anything—it was clearly a profound, honest, and hopeful wish for a deeply troubled country. It was then that I really got it. I was moved to the core and choked with tears: The emotional connections one can have with art are much more powerful than anything else we can surround ourselves with in our environments and daily lives. Ever since, I have committed myself to finding those connections. Emotions, both of the senses and the soul, became my mantra when looking at art for my own collection, and later, for the pieces I would suggest to my clients. Since I'm inspired by so many different things—places, travel, people, and obviously art—I wanted to give my company a name that had a broader and deeper connotation than just interior design, or art, or decor. My style is an amalgam of different perspectives that all work together. I envisioned my clients living with the things they loved, with the colors that inspired them, and with amazing art on the walls, entertaining guests in a fun and stimulating environment. Each person, couple, or family is different. I didn't see any reason people's homes should look the same or why people could not have unique pieces of art displayed on their walls. People's lives and personalities are usually not beige. Why then should their homes be confined to one style or color? I wanted something both dynamic and fluid, so I created my own verb from the noun and adjective "lifestyle," and called my company "Lifestyling® by Maria Gabriela Brito." A few months after, I trademarked the word "Lifestyling" and it became an asset of my business, too. It has been a privilege and a dream to be invited into my clients' homes in an intimate and personal way. I really get to know what they love and need, and I'm always willing to go the extra mile for them, such as taking a plane to pick up a piece in Paris or Mexico City, if that is what is required. I'm happy to meet with anonymous graffiti artists in the middle of the night to commission pieces for my clients, or negotiate with furniture dealers in Ankara on the telephone at 6:00 a.m., if that's what it takes. I'm as comfortable in flea markets and thrift shops as in such high-end galleries as Gagosian, or art fairs like Art Basel Miami Beach. Life is not a box limited by four sides. We don't live in compartmentalized areas, and people's homes should not be, either. Contemporary art should be an integral part of people's lives, and what better way to make that happen than to live with it? And who says that an edgy piece of art can't be paired with an antique piece found in a thrift shop? Since I didn't have much when I started my business, I ventured into it with the images of my own apartment and art collection as my calling card. The first rendition of my apartment was published in ten different magazines all over the world from Hong Kong to Dubai (and even landed on the cover of *DCasa,* one of Brazil's most prestigious interior design magazines). Throughout the life of "Lifestyling®" I've had several extraordinary moments and milestones that have given me the impetus to be even more creative and to enhance the experience that I give my clients. From time to time, I like to explore different media, as in 2010, when I designed an interactive ebook and "coloring book" for children that narrates and illustrates the life of the Mexican artist Frida Kahlo.

OPPOSITE "Frida's World," the app that I designed for iPads and iPhones, opens with this virtual "cover." I worked really closely with the illustrator, Natalie Morales, to make sure she understood Frida Kahlo in the same way I did.

ABOVE RIGHT, FROM TOP A photograph by the Brazilian-French collective, Assume Vivid Astro Focus, hangs in a foyer; an abstract oil by Venezuelan-Italian artist Vladimiro Politano was placed above a demi-lune table from a Paris flea market; a sexy photograph by New York artist Marilyn Minter is a surprise behind the stove.

FINDING BEAUTY AND INSPIRATION

I have dared to be different and be inspired by things everywhere. Besides contemporary art, I look for visual stimulation and emotional connection from people, movies, places, and fashion. Who says that an entire room can't be inspired by Frida Kahlo's life, Marc Jacob's runway collection, or Sophia Loren's movies? My muses, the ones on these pages, all share a strong personal presence. They also all have (or had) very interesting inner lives. I always trust my instincts and my sharp freedom of association. Sometimes I ask: Why have I chosen this pattern or color combination? And later, I can bring back the personality, piece of clothing, or movie set from which I took my first cue to start a project. Sometimes my clients are my inspiration. Everything flows from their colorful lives. My goal is to create spaces and develop contemporary art collections that help people dream, talk, fantasize and, above all, be excited about their lives—and about coming home every night. Strong, iconic women who have left their creative marks on the world constantly inspire my life and my work. Being unique and able to present one's style with conviction is a true art. These women are inspirational not only because of the way they present themselves to the world, but because of their personalities, their strong spirits, and their capacities to make others dream. Frida Kahlo, with her Tehuana outfits, multi-colored ribbons, braided hair, rings of silver and semi-precious stones on every finger, and most importantly, her raw and compelling art, was one of the first iconic women to have an influence on me. Kahlo said, "I do not know whether my paintings are surrealist or not, but I do know that they are the frankest expression of myself." Her life, marked by dramatic events, was immortalized in her art, which became at once self-expression and autobiography. She shows up quite often in my projects. In Mexico, I have bought hand-crafted boxes with Kahlo's image, and for a client's bedroom, I designed a headboard upholstered with a fabric depicting small images of Kahlo in vibrant colors. Carmen Miranda, who so successfully packaged the idea of Brazilian-chic, and crafted an image brand from colorful and lush fruits, high-platform sandals, and a fearless attitude, and Josephine Baker, who danced around the world with a skirt of sequined bananas, made me think about the importance of developing a distinctive personal style and sticking to it. Mademoiselle Gabrielle Chanel—the famous Coco—is also a source of inspiration: Her high standards of design and craftsmanship helped her, her brand, and her legacy survive world wars, lovers, and exiles. A century later, the name Chanel still prevails in a world that is oversaturated with labels and designers. Chanel had a very clear idea of the female model, one based on her own lifestyle and experience, from her apartment to her clothes. Another extraordinary fashion designer who has left her mark on my world is Diane von Furstenberg. She created the Wrap Dress in 1972, which landed on the cover of *Newsweek* three years after five million of the chic and comfortable dresses were sold. A muse of artists Andy Warhol and Chuck Close, a social figure embraced by Studio 54, and a symbol of all things New York, including the revival of the Meatpacking

Sophia Loren

Gwyneth Paltrow

Penélope Cruz

Diane von Furstenberg

District and the opening of the Highline, von Furstenberg looks carefree but polished, regal yet nurturing. She is a perfect combination of the attitude I aim to translate into my designs. Iris Apfel is a spectacular New Yorker who is now 90 years old and still making heads turn. Mixing Lanvin dresses with ethnic beaded bracelets and necklaces, there's nothing conventional about Apfel. The Costume Institute at the Metropolitan Museum of Art in New York celebrated Apfel's style with a show of her best outfits, and MAC launched a line of cosmetics inspired by her. It's not a secret that I love going to the movies, and it doesn't matter to me if the film is silent, independent, international, Hollywood, animated, or a documentary. Three actresses who have all won Academy Awards never fail to inspire me: Sophia Loren, Gwyneth Paltrow, and Penélope Cruz. Their inner and outer beauty, their poise and sophistication, and their gifts for delivering moving performances have made these women my heroines. For more than five decades, Sophia Loren has captured the eyes of the world by being unapologetically sexy, classy, and independent. Her style in many of her movies is timeless. Gwyneth Paltrow is exceptionally beautiful, inside and out. She is a multi-talented Renaissance woman, skilled at everything she does. Having the pleasure of knowing her personally, I can say that her generosity and fantastic spirit make her someone I truly admire. I have been a fan of hers ever since I saw her as Viola in *Shakespeare in Love*, but Marge in *The Talented Mr. Ripley,* Margot in *The Royal Tenenbaums,* and Catherine in *Proof* have also clicked with me. Many of Paltrow's movies have prompted me to look for images and stills long after I have left the theater. Away from the big screen, Paltrow walks the red carpet in a white Tom Ford gown with the same ease, grace, and poise as she does running down the streets of London in Isabel Marant. It's impossible to have more style. Penélope Cruz is the embodiment of the sexy, fearless, and stylish Spanish woman. She is a muse of both directors Pedro Almodóvar and Woody Allen, and I have watched her movies in awe ever since Bigas Lunas's acclaimed *Jamón Jamón* was released in 1992. Her performances as Raimunda in *Volver* and Maria Elena in *Vicky Cristina Barcelona* have encouraged me to make two trips to Spain: first to Madrid, then to Barcelona.

ABOVE LEFT I'm so grateful to have met some of the women I think are extraordinary and, in some cases, to have collaborated with them professionally.

OPPOSITE Guillermo Kahlo took this photograph of his daughter Frida Kahlo in 1932. On my first trip to New York, in the Spring of 1983, I discovered her work at the Grey Art Gallery at New York University, her first retrospective outside of Mexico. My parents and I experienced the mysterious self-portraits of a woman with thick eyebrows and abundant hair, the magnetic colors, the Mexican folk figures, and the fruits and animals. Ever since, I have been fascinated by her life and her art.

ART-À-PORTER

Fashion has always been a source of inspiration for me. I'm always excited to have both established and emerging designers rock my world. I believe that while it's important to have a certain style and to own it, one can also play with fashion in a creative way that incorporates and reflects aspects of people's personalities and that suits different moods on various occasions. Fabrics, proportions, materials, accessories, patterns, and color combinations have all had a definite impact on the way I put together my designs. In my rooms, references to fashion can be found in the choice of rugs, pillows, accessories, and especially, wallpaper. I believe that fashion is art; Alexander McQueen, Christian Lacroix, Marc Jacobs, Rodarte, Jean Paul Gaultier, and Karl Lagerfeld for Chanel have all treated the runways like major art installations. Isabel Marant is my go-to designer, both for inspiration and for my day-to-day clothing. She has made her label an unprecedented success without too much fuss or over-the-top creations, by staying true to her style, and easily capturing the *je ne sais quoi* of the Parisian Left Bank: Boho-chic, wearable, and unique. I'm always dying to see what Marant comes up with next. I am inspired by the fearless pattern-on-pattern combinations she creates, where tie-dyed red jackets are perfectly coupled with a pair of light yellow and grey snake-printed jeans. It's that kind of bravery that I go after when designing a room. Not everyone is willing to go that far, and although sometimes I'm perfectly fine with that, I try to push my clients to go beyond what they think they are comfortable with. People like Marc Jacobs, for example, who have created fashion and fantasy at different levels of affordability, earn my utmost respect. I was incredibly taken by his 2011 Spring/Summer collection, with its large hibiscus belts and the orange, ochre, carmine, brick, and eggplant color palette. The gorgeous zigzag patterns and glittery sandals keep me dreaming and have undoubtedly influenced my designs. Domenico Dolce and Stefano Gabbana, who consistently deliver heightened renditions of what Italy means to them, with bold colors and designs that can make even fabrics printed with whimsical motifs like tomatoes and peppers into the sexiest things in the world. I'm also a great fan of fashion photography, and when the space and the client come together, there's nothing more beautiful than a Richard Avedon or a Helmut Newton photograph. Sometimes, fashion photography is downright edgy, and if my clients allow me, I look at David Drebin, Marilyn Minter, Sante D'Orazio, or Christa Joo Hyun D'Angelo for the perfect piece.

A FEW WORDS ON BEAUTY There are some fundamental pillars in what I do: I help my clients start or develop contemporary art collections, I design spaces where such art can be displayed and where I blend furniture pieces and accessories together, and I bring the personalities and experiences of my clients to their homes, all while trying to achieve a state of harmony and beauty. I don't mean to say that everything inside a home should be beautiful—sometimes what is beautiful to me is not beautiful to someone else—but aesthetics play a very important role in what I do. Although it's true that beauty is in the eye of the beholder, we can't deny that there are certain artworks, objects, places, buildings, and cities that are considered more beautiful than others. While some things might be described as interesting, quirky, thought-provoking, or fun, they are not necessarily beautiful. Regardless of what critics, cynics, thinkers, or anti-establishment types might say, people the world over crave beauty—beauty that invites contemplation. Beauty provides joy. Beauty makes people happy. Beauty feeds the soul. I do not know anyone who would not like to live surrounded by beautiful things. It may be a cliché, but it's no wonder Paris is the most visited place in the world: It's an extraordinarily beautiful city, with streets, buildings, museums, squares, parks, restaurants, and shops that, for the most part, celebrate beauty. It's enormously powerful for human beings to carry with them memories of beautiful things or places, no matter where they live or how long it takes them to see something similar again. Visual stimulation of this kind stays imprinted on the mind, whether it comes from a trip to a foreign country or from an art exhibit, providing a respite for even the busiest person. This powerful state of mind can be multiplied tenfold if we live with beauty, if we do not have to take a flight to Paris, and if we can readily access it in our immediate environment. There is also the question of beauty and art. Should all art be beautiful? I don't think so. I believe that there's always room for reactionary movements, for artists who want to create for the purpose of conveying a strong idea, for opposing a regime, or for expressing rage, anger, or grief. I have objects and some artworks that aren't necessarily beautiful but recall a memory, a note of humor, or an aspect of who I am. It's the combination, the sum of all the parts, that, in my opinion, produces something that is beautiful. Fortunately, there are plenty of fashion designers, artists, jewelers, furniture-makers, designers of objects, and those who, like me, have the ability to put all the pieces together and who thereby seek to create beauty.

ABOVE The world of fashion is completely intertwined with the world of art. Fashion is drama, fantasy, and splendor. The dress by D&G, a line by Dolce & Gabbana, from the 2012 Spring/Summer collection, is inspired by vintage scarves and other fabrics found in the archives of Domenico Dolce and Stefano Gabbana.

Prada, Milan

With Iris Apfel

With Sarah Easley

Pucci pillows

With Christy Turlington

Edition 01, Qatar

Isabel Marant

With Marc Jacobs

I'm moved by the genius of Marc Jacobs, the magic of Isabel Marant, the exuberance of Dolce & Gabbana, the vision of Beth Buccini and Sarah Easley, the beauty of models—like Christy Turlington and Elettra Rossellini Weidemann—who have traveled around the world and have become the muses and ambassadors for humanitarian causes. I'm also motivated by the brilliance of hip-hop moguls like Sean Combs, who has both impeccable style and a sharp eye, and who can also successfully design entire fashion lines.

Dolce & Gabbana

With Sean Combs

Marc Jacobs

Kirna Zabête, New York

With Elettra Wiedermann

With Beth Buccini

MY HOME: MY CANVAS

With one-year-old Daniel

My house is my autobiography. A house is never really done, and mine certainly isn't. It keeps morphing as my interests change and evolve, along with those of my family. Most people are a combination of different experiences—an accumulation of travels, interests, passions, and certain moments in time. That is what my house represents to me. I certainly do not subscribe to one style or another. Rather, I like mixing and combining furniture and accessories from different periods, and somehow, they all come together. I like daring colors and style combinations, and I love fun, stylish wallpaper that also makes a statement. Not everything I have has an illustrious provenance, but everything I have says something about who I am. I have thrift-shop finds, like the cabinet where we keep our wine glasses and Champagne flutes, which is next to an almost seven-foot-high canvas by the Brazilian street artists Os Gêmeos, and my Art Deco chairs upholstered in an orange fabric from Senegal. To me, designing comes very instinctively and intuitively, and sometimes—even if I really don't know where I'm going to place something, I just know that it belongs in my house or in one of my clients' homes, if I'm buying for them. I love vintage and antique pieces as much as I love mid-twentieth–century modern and contemporary design. Sometimes I even like kitschy items, such as pillows with the profile of the Queen of England, which I had in the first version of my family room, next to a chair covered in a fabric with a pattern of the British Union Jack. Later, I traded those pillows for some fabulous ones, with brightly colored fabrics by the Scandinavian designer Josef Frank. I switched an acrylic coffee table for an extraordinary rainbow ottoman designed by Donna Wilson. To me, it is also important to have a sense of humor when designing. I have gathered objects from all of my travels around the world. My black springstone sculpture was found in a garden in South Africa, close to the Cape of Good Hope, which is at the southernmost tip of Africa. The Malawians who majestically carved the stone are delightful people and opened their shop for me on a Saturday, even though that is when they celebrate their religious service, just so I could purchase the piece. We sent it to New York in a container, not really knowing if and when we were going to get it. But we took a leap of faith and did receive it a couple of months later. I placed it on top of a large oak trunk, and every time I see it, I think about the vastness and beauty of Africa. I have carried dishes, tables, chairs, books, vases, trays, toys, canvases, and pretty much anything I love, from Paris, Athens, Capri, Miami, Caracas, London, Rome, and Cape Town. I have designed and planned my house in a way that is accommodating to everyone in my family. I transformed one of the hallway closets into a wine cellar for my husband, Marcio, who is a wine collector and who has completed several levels of sommelier courses. It has a system for cooling and humidity control, insulated walls, and controlled-temperature lights. Marcio's wine collection is quite extensive, and by making the diamond-shaped bins and other racks double depth, he has great storage capacity. My two sons, Daniel and Oliver, enjoy lots of playtime in the television room and in their bedroom, which has a bunk bed with a pole to climb up or slide down from. I have a large walk-in closet that I love, and my home office—my sanctuary—is where I spend hours thinking, creating, and dreaming. My collection of contemporary art is very meaningful to me. It has been years in the making and has evolved with me. For the most part, all the pieces I own were created in the past 15 years or so, with about roughly a third of them by Latin American artists. Every piece has a lot of soul

and represents different stages in my life. I feel happy when I see these artworks, either because they remind me of the artist with whom I have a personal connection, or because they recall a moment in my life. When I think about my collection, part of its appeal includes its different media and techniques. I have pieces that are mixed media on canvas and on wood; neon; oil and acrylic on canvas; C-prints and digital C-prints; drawings, etchings, and silkscreens; and small sculptures of poured resin and polyurethane. I also think it makes sense to make groupings by geographic regions: In the hot Latin group, I have collected several works by Vik Muniz, Assume Vivid Astro Focus or AVAF, Flavia Da Rin, and Os Gêmeos. In the French group of artists, I have works by Nicolas Pichon, Corinne Dalle-Ore, and an artist who goes by the name of Joseph, which all share similar characteristics. Their techniques are mostly mixed media with a color palette of reds, hot pinks, oranges, and turquoises. I also have a great canvas by Jean-Marc Dallanegra, who is French, but whose technique and style has very little relation to the works of the other Gallic artists who share the walls of my apartment with him. In the American group, besides Joseph Piccillo, there's the versatile Marc Bradford, the disco-queen Mickalene Thomas, the multi-talented Joe Grillo, the sensuous Pamela Hanson, the legendary Kenny Scharf, the rising star Christa Joo Hyun D'Angelo, the witty Chen Chen, and the genius of FAILE. Then there are two pieces that I call the "power-nations." One is by the German photographer Rafael Neff, and the other by the Dutch photographer Ruud van Empel. Although they are still very young, my kids know a lot about art. Their bedroom is also a place in which I hang and display art. I added a very cool photograph of the amusement park at Coney Island by Italian artist Luigi Visconti and a series of prints in different sizes and shapes by such artists as Scharf and the Miami collective "FriendsWithYou." I also collect books, and probably have more than 800—from novels that take me far away from the world I live in, to management and business books that I learn from, to oversize photography, travel, architecture, fashion, and art books that help me dream. I love and collect costume jewelry, and each piece somehow inspires my designs. The shape of a semi-precious stone, the wild color combinations, the intricacies of the engraving, or the braided bracelets in ethnic materials all bring something to my creative process. On the contemporary side, I love the designs of Lynn Ban, Miu Miu, Marni, Ysharia, Eddie Borgo, Dolce & Gabbana, and Philippe Audibert. In vintage pieces, Schiaparelli, Chanel, Dior, Miriam Haskell, and Yves Saint Laurent designed chic and stimulating pieces that I treasure, love to wear, and get inspired by, time and time again.

OPPOSITE In the hallway off the foyer, I hung an acrylic-mounted self portrait by Argentinian artist Flavia Da Rin over an antique demi-lune wood table on which I placed some of my favorite books, a Jonathan Adler pottery horse, and an 1980s pop-inspired sculpture I found on eBay. I discovered the Da Rin at the Art Basel Miami Beach fair in 2010 and fell in love with her work immediately. After shaking hands with the dealers, I left the convention center with the piece under my arm—something quite unheard of. The fact that the photograph was round made it even more appealing for my collection, in which all the wall-hung pieces are usually either rectangular or square. The piece had just returned from shows in Rio de Janeiro and São Paulo, Brazil, where the curators of the Banco do Brasil had selected the best Argentinean talents in contemporary art to be part of the exhibits.

RIGHT I love the strength, movement, and power that the painting of horses by upstate New York artist Joseph Piccillo conveys. The piece is over eight feet long and six feet high, and was such a large canvas that it didn't fit in the elevator, or up the stairway, of my building. I had to send it back to the gallery where it was taken off its frame, to be reattached once inside my apartment. It was all worth it. Its impact on the whole living room is undeniable.

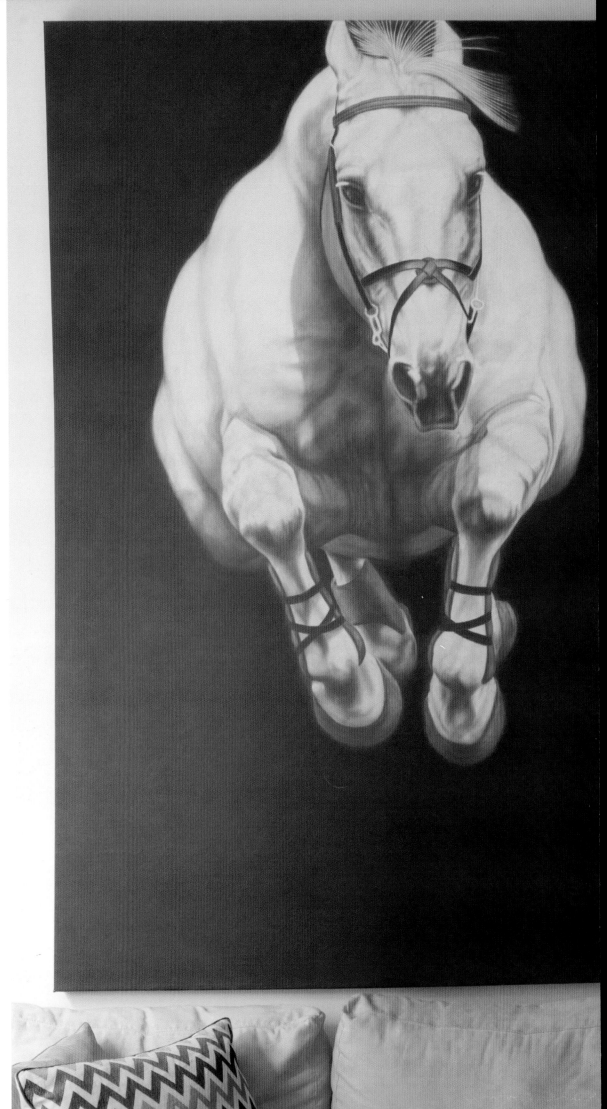

RIGHT Pieces by Os Gêmeos are so rare and I am such a fan that when I found this canvas in a gallery in Milan, Italy, I didn't think twice. I had to have it. It's called *Quando o Cuco Aprende a Voar*, which means *When the Cuckoo Learns How to Fly* and, along with the other work by the Brazilian twin brothers, exemplifies the themes they explore: the dreams, yearnings, and desires for a better life of the people in Brazil who live in poverty. In the living room, the painting hangs behind two Art Deco chairs that came covered in a Senegalese orange fabric with ochre stripes. The pillows are made of Burmese saris. On the left is the Springstone sculpture I bought in the Cape of Good Hope in South Africa. At right, I placed a sculpture from AVAF that was made from one of the original voting booths from the 2000 Presidential elections in Dade County, Florida. The booth is covered with a special paper that changes color and shape when the accompanying masks are worn.

LEFT On top of some of my art books, between the Art Deco chairs, I placed a plate with balloon dogs that is a take off of one of American artist Jeff Koons' sculptures.

OPPOSITE I found the extraordinary ottoman, which is now in my television room, at The Future Perfect, a shop in New York and Brooklyn. It is by Scottish designer Donna Wilson and is made of a rainbow-colored jersey fabric. The navy and white rug that anchors the room is by the New York-based designer Madeline Weinrib. The child-sized Lou Lou chair by French designer Philippe Starck, for Kartell, is the right size for my boys to sit on to draw at the table. When the kids are not playing, a wonderful jelly-like vase by Italian designer Gaetano Pesce, sits on a tray decorated with a pattern by the Scandinavian designer Josef Frank. Luckily, both are immune to spills.

OVERLEAF I have always admired Scandinavian designers, so when I found out that Just Scandinavian, a now mainly online source, carried a large selection of pillows covered with Josef Frank fabrics, I got a bunch of them, all in different patterns. Frank's designs are fantastic and reflect his travels around the world, and, with exotic names like Teheran, Primavera, Brazil, La Plata, and Manhattan; his textiles and wallpapers won me over many years ago. On the wall is a large C-print by the German artist Rafael Neff, and the chair covered with the Union Jack-patterned fabric was custom-made. The leather "Love" pillow is from Maison de Vacances, a French home-design company. A collection of Andy Warhol skateboards sit on the windowsill. I had actually bought a set for one of my clients and loved it so much that I got one for myself.

LEFT I keep part of my large collection of books in the home office. I love to browse through the images in them when I need an energy boost, or to kick-start my creativity. The vintage chair has been reupholstered with a bolero-inspired Middle Eastern suzani fabric. The figurine—the Little Wanderer—is a multiple by the contemporary Japanese artist Yoshitomo Nara.

BELOW LEFT The retro patterned wallpaper in the master bedroom was inspired by 1970s designs. Called Dandelion Clocks, it is from the English company Sanderson. The etched and glazed aqua-colored lamp is a vintage piece.

OPPOSITE I chose a palette of turquoises and yellows for the master bedroom, as the colors feel optimistic without being overwhelming. For a long time, I could not find the perfect piece of art for the room—then I came across this sexy screen print by the Brooklyn, New York-based artist Mickalene Thomas. It's called *Can't We Just Sit Down and Talk It Over?* Like Thomas, I'm obsessed with vintage textiles and the style, fashion, and music of the 1970s. The headboard, upholstered in beige suede, was custom-made. The colorful pillows are by the Scottish designer Morag Macpherson. The vintage suzani is from an Istanbul flea market.

OVERLEAF I stumbled upon this neon sculpture by Korean-American artist Christa Joo Hyun D'Angelo at the preview of the Volta Art Fair in New York in 2012. As with many of my art purchases, I knew right away that I really wanted it. I had an epiphany: The artist wanted to show clearly how, in our society, we always want more and are unstoppable in our cravings to fulfill our desires. This time, though, my own desire won me over and *Desire* came home with me. Some of my extensive selection of costume jewelry has been arranged on the tray.

My boys' current bedroom reflects who they are. It is fun, colorful, and joyous. I also wanted my sons to have their own experiences living with contemporary art, so I listened to their opinions when selecting the pieces in the room.

FAR LEFT The Blue Rope Meltdown chair by British designer Tom Price is from the Industry Gallery in Washington, D.C. It was created by almost melting a polypropylene rope inside a seat-shaped mold. Amazingly, no other materials were used. The limited-edition photograph is by the Italian artist Luigi Visconti.

LEFT The bunk bed is by CedarWorks, a company based in Maine that manufactures furniture exclusively built on the concept of functionality and play. The bed keeps my kids entertained for hours. The pillows recall American artist Robert Indiana's Numbers series, and the blue lamp is from Kartell.

BELOW FAR LEFT The limited-edition print entitled *Cosmic Donut* is by Kenny Scharf. The limited-edition print on the left below is by FriendsWithYou, an art collective based in Miami, Florida, and the one to the right is by the contemporary realist artist Robert Jackson, both of which were made in collaboration with LittleCollector.com. The wallpaper is by Morag Macpherson.

LEFT The limited edition prints are by Larry Moss, *top*, a New York artist who works exclusively with latex balloons; and Sonni, *bottom*, an Argentinean artist. Both were produced for LittleCollector.com. The polka-dot pumpkins on the windowsill are Cerealart multiples by Yayoi Kusama, a contemporary Japanese artist.

OPPOSITE My kids keep their toys and projects organized—sort of—in two storage units from Oeuf, a New York company. The metal boxes are from 100drine, a French designer, and the large fabric-covered containers are from Italian company Foppapedretti.

ABOVE My son Daniel and I enjoy a day at the Tibidabo Amusement Park in Barcelona, in the summer of 2011.

RIGHT I was unprepared for the overwhelming love that motherhood brought to my life. Daniel, right, and Oliver are my greatest teachers. Seeing the world from their vantage point and approaching each day with their sense of humor is a blessing. They have started their own collection of toy cars. Like mother, like sons. I guess the apples don't fall far from the tree.

THE ART OF ENTERTAINING

Entertaining can be fun and effortless. I love my house, I love my friends, and I love having people over. Living in a city as compact as New York City helps a lot since it takes a relatively short amount of time to go from one end of the island to the other, and people can gather easily for drinks or dinner without having a long commute. I put most of my creativity into setting a memorable table. I'm a fan of gorgeous plates that make a statement. When I got married, one of the gifts from my registry that I loved the most was a complete set of 24 Versace plates for Rosenthal, decorated with a fantastic design of copious fruits, flowers, and a regal gold rim. Thinking back, I could have chosen something a lot edgier, but I still treasure the plates because they are so meaningful to me. Throughout the years, I have collected plates by Italian artist and designer Piero Fornasetti, from the Mexican company DFC, and even melamine plates from the National Gallery of Art in London that were produced in collaboration with Whitbread Wilkinson, a British design company. I got so excited when I found these last ones because not only were they inexpensive, but they can be used in so many ways, including informal dinner parties or picnics. The entire collection shows details from paintings at the National Gallery, but my favorite is the one of the Emperor Napoleon I by Emile-Jean-Horace Vernet. Besides plates, I have also collected Indian beaded placemats, glass and wood centerpieces, embroidered fabrics, vintage colored glasses, hand-blown candleholders, vintage Bakelite serving pieces, and a bunch of cool coffee and espresso cups and saucers. When setting the table, consistent in the style of everything I do, I usually place many different kinds of pieces together, since I don't like a look where everything matches. Finally, I put lots of flowers in differently shaped and colored vases around the house. I do have one rule: each vase must have an arrangement with only one type of flower, unless it's one of those amazing arrangements by a professional florist, which I personally have no idea how to create. So, it's either a bunch of red roses, a stem of orchids, or a dramatic composition of calla lilies, all of which I usually find at my local deli. I'm not that fabulous in the kitchen, but my husband is a great cook. If he's not available, I'll do a take-out and delivery party. We serve wine almost all of the time, since one of the pleasures of having a wine collection is sharing it with friends. However, my absolute favorite drink of all is Champagne. I don't use it to celebrate a special occasion, but rather as just another type of wine, which it actually is. I find that it pairs well with almost any type of food.

A WORD ON CHAMPAGNE Real Champagne is from the Champagne region in France. Prosecco, Cava, and all the other bubbly and sparkling wines are not Champagne but are usually made using the *Méthode Champenoise*. The sweetness in Champagne is categorized by terminology created in the nineteenth century: "Extra dry" for Champagne that is really sweet, almost nonexistent today, and "Brut" for a drier and less sugary version. Everything else is referred to with newer terminology, like demi-sec or Extra Brut, though it is not really used by the top *negociants*—the growers and producers of Champagne in France. Almost all of the bottles produced in Champagne are excellent wines. However, among the most extraordinary ones, I would lean toward anything from Bollinger, Taittinger, Krug, Gosset, Louis Roederer, and Veuve Fourney et Fils—it is impossible to go wrong with any of these. Because Champagne is very versatile, I would recommend pairing any Brut Champagne with the following foods: all Asian food, sushi in particular; risotto or pasta with creamy sauces, or even simpler ones such as *cacio e pepe*, or cheese and pepper; lightly prepared fish and seafood; and hard cheeses, such as Manchego, parmesan, or gouda. But stay away from anything with tomatoes in it, as the acidity in both the tomatoes and the Champagne will spoil the taste of everything. Last but not least: how and where to serve your Champagne. The correct temperature should be about 45 degrees Fahrenheit, and the bottle can be chilled in a bucket filled half with ice and half with water for about half an hour. If you want to chill a bottle in the refrigerator, don't leave it there for more than three or four hours. To serve Champagne, traditionally, I love to use flutes. However, research indicates that Champagne is best experienced in a shape reminiscent of a regular wine glass, as that shape enhances the bubbles, aroma, and taste. For a change, use a tulip-shaped red wine glass to see if it makes a big difference to you. Hands down, the Austrian Riedel company makes the best wine glasses: The difference in taste from these glasses is really substantial.

ABOVE My favorite wines, *top*, consist of a selection of both aged and young vintages. Our wine cellar, which I built inside a closet, *center*, has a cooling system and a rack that can hold more than 500 bottles. My table is set with plates by Fernando and Humberto Campana, *bottom*.

OPPOSITE I found this vintage cabinet in a thrift shop on the Upper East Side, soon after I arrived in New York in 2000. It is especially convenient for entertaining, as I store some of our glassware in it. On top, I placed a print by AVAF, some favorite art books, and two epoxy-resin hams created by the Brooklyn-based artist Chen Chen. I also displayed a small collection of wooden dolls by the American designer Alexander Girard, which represent a lot of what I'm about. They are playful, dreamy, and fun toys that have the strength to be either pieces of art or everyday objects. They combine images that Girard had gathered on his trips to Central America and Italy with the genius of Scandinavian design, of which I'm also a big fan.

There's something about beautifully designed plates that makes me happy, either because they are used to gather people around a table to share a meal, or because I'm excited by their fabulous patterns! I have several sets of dishes that I mix and match when I'm entertaining. The dessert plates by Laurie Simmons, *above*, with their cakes, cookies, candies, and pies, are just brilliant. Mickalene Thomas' limited edition melamine plates are also trays, *left* and *right*. Each design is from Thomas' collection of textiles and wallcoverings. The Love plate from Arjang & Company is by Robert Indiana, *below left*, and the bright yellow whimsical one, *below right*, is by Yayoi Kusama. The simplicity of Alexander Girard's designs, *below*, are captivating. The Bernardaud plates, *opposite*, are by the Brazilian designers Fernando and Humberto Campana. The china was created using images from their furniture, and multiplying them to form a collage. How genius is that? The cutlery is 1970s Bakelite, and the gorgeous centerpiece is by Gaetano Pesce for Meritalia. The still life painting, a gift from my father, was bought from the Syrian artist Antonio Haydar Mardelli, who lived in Caracas for a while.

ABOVE One of a collection of plates aptly named MexICON, as the images depict famous Mexican personalities, bears the face of Andrés García, a Mexican soap opera star from the 1980s who was wildly popular in Venezuela when I was growing up.

RIGHT In our building, we have a terrace that is perfect for summer soirées and early fall wine tastings. Of course, styling the table is my favorite part of the pre-party stage. When I found the plates by the Mexican company DFC at The Future Perfect, I was transported back to my childhood. I paired the plates with a hand-embroidered fabric made by the Otomi Mexican Indians, which is used as a tablecloth. The vase is by Italian architect Gaetano Pesce, the napkins came from a flea market in New York, and the tumblers are vintage. There is a lightness and sense of humor about this table that really makes me happy. *Voilà!* The table is set with a Champagne bucket and all. For me, there's no party or gathering without Champagne. To further the mix of colors and cultures, I added a suzani-inspired outdoor rug and a set of multicolor solar lanterns that get powered up during the day and stay lit at night on their own.

ABOVE I found a small shop in Playa del Carmen, Mexico, that had racks of colorful serapes.

RIGHT The inspired set-up for an outdoor party is Bohemian-chic. September and October are the last opportunities for al fresco dinners in New York, but as the sun starts to set earlier, it can get chilly at night. I don't want my guests to be cold, which is why I scatter blankets all around. The rug is a vintage Mexican serape, as is the blanket on the back of the sofa. The wrap on the chair to the left was hand-painted in Africa. The horses on the table are Swedish, the blue vase is from the Czech Republic, the Champagne cups are vintage, and the towels on the table are from Missoni.

Collecti
Contempo
and the Extr
World

A UNIVERSE OF GALLERIES

The best places to start learning about collecting contemporary art are local galleries. Although they might sometimes seem intimidating, they present new shows every four to six weeks, allowing people who are really interested in becoming collectors or just buying a good piece of art for the first time to learn a lot about art movements, trends, artists, and the current art market. Although a lot of the galleries on my list show very expensive works, they are all worth a visit, even if it is just to look around. When embarking on collecting contemporary art, it is a good idea to start educating one's eye by starting at the top. Galleries around the world operate in a variety of ways. I'm most familiar with those in New York, London, and Paris, where I have bought the most pieces for both my clients and myself. Other cities currently bursting with contemporary art galleries include Berlin, Barcelona, São Paulo, Mexico City, Los Angeles, Hong Kong, and Shanghai. Top-tier galleries usually have a program for artists whose careers they want to support and develop, acting as their agents to establish relationships with museum curators, art critics, writers, editors, and collectors. Such galleries help artists get monographs on their work published, point them in the right direction to apply for grants and residencies, and help them get the recognition that is sometimes hard for them to get on their own. When an artist releases a work to the gallery to be offered to any potential buyer for the first time, that piece of art is part of what is called the primary market. On the other hand, if somebody has owned a piece before and he or she is trying to resell it through a gallery, then that piece becomes part of the secondary market. This distinction becomes important for a few reasons: A brand new piece that comes straight from the gallery to the market usually has a set price that has not been increased or altered by the factors that play a role in secondary market transactions. For example, if the piece is part of a series, one would want to know if it has been sold out. Is it part of an edition, or one-of-a-kind? What is its background? Does it belong to an important phase in the artist's career? Has it been exhibited in a museum show? What is its current condition? All of these issues are taken into account when pricing a piece in the secondary market. There is a very high-end tier of galleries in New York, most of them in the Chelsea area, that I love and respect. A lot of the artists represented in these galleries are mid-career or established, and in some cases, they are part of the estates of deceased artists. Prices can be astronomical, but the galleries also offer work by younger talents, which tend to be more accessible. Most of these galleries also have a selection of works on paper, prints, and limited editions, which are a good way to start a collection at a relatively low price point. There is another group of galleries that is much more accessible and represents a great variety of emerging artists—meaning

that regardless of his or her age, the artist is within the first five years of his or her art career—who are waiting to be discovered. On the Lower East Side and in the East Village, galleries with an edge are having a creative renaissance similar to that in the early 1980s. SoHo, NoHo, and TriBeCa also have their share of good galleries, as do Williamsburg and DUMBO, in Brooklyn. Galleries on the Upper East Side deal mostly with the secondary market.

LEFT AND BELOW LEFT When I designed this lounge for the pop-up gallery of French-American artist Alexander Charriol in a huge 5,000 square-foot space across the street from Madison Square Park in Manhattan, I drew an incredible amount of inspiration from my trips to Paris. I wanted to create a contrast between the amazing contemporary art that Charriol creates and the sparseness of the venue. My goal was to design something comfortable, chic, and unique, which I accomplished by integrating French antique furniture, oriental rugs, and flea market finds, while leaving the industrial details of the space exposed. Charriol's show and pop-up gallery was a success, and the opening night party drew more than 500 guests, including models, celebrities, and art critics.

LEFT I'm pointing to one of the mesmerizing pieces that artist E.V. Day shot while at the Foundation Claude Monet at Giverny in France. The subject, naked and body-painted in each of the photographs in the show, was punk-rock performer Kembra Pfahler. In the spring of 2012, Kathy Grayson and her team at the Hole Gallery in New York put on a truly spectacular exhibit where they replicated Monet's famous gardens at Giverny, complete with an artificial pond.

LEFT In the summer of 2012, the Hole Gallery had an opening of artist Holton Rower's solo show. Holton, the grandson of the American artist Alexander Calder, has developed an innovative technique. He pours paint onto shaped plywood panels to which he has previously added protrusions or obstacles so that the paint is forced to flow around them, creating striking zigzags, waterfalls, and endless streams of colors.

OPPOSITE A solo show of the work of Dutch artists and industrial designers Tejo Remy and René Veenhuizen took place at the Industry Gallery in Washington, D.C., in 2010. *Growth Bench* is completely made of tennis balls. At the back of the space, the artists designed a maquette of an outdoor club house made of Accoya, an all-weather wood that does not age, splinter, or crack.

Below are of some of my favorite galleries around the world.

NEW YORK

Sikkema Jenkins & Company:
One of the things I love about this gallery is that there is still only one. Located in a large and beautiful building in Chelsea, it operates on a relatively small scale while being very influential. Sikkema has an enviable stable of artists that ranges from Vik Muniz to Kara Walker and Mark Bradford. The gallery is passionate about sharing the details, facts, and anecdotes behind the artworks of all of their artists.

Lehmann Maupin Gallery:
Located in two large spaces, one in Chelsea and an edgier one on the Lower East Side, the gallery represents Tracey Emin, Hernan Bas, Mickalene Thomas, Adriana Varejão, and Gilbert & George, among many other very established artists. It also frequently hosts collective shows with works by an array of artists from all over the world. The owners, Rachel Lehmann and David Maupin, are friendly, flexible, and open-minded.

Gladstone Gallery:
Barbara Gladstone is not a gallerist—she is an institution. As one of the most respected and serious dealers in the industry, and a woman with great poise and sophistication, Gladstone treats her artists and their careers with strategy and care. Both of her spaces in Chelsea are very impressive. Some of my favorites there include Wangechi Mutu, Matthew Barney, and the estate of Keith Haring.

Paul Kasmin Gallery:
Paul Kasmin has assembled a fascinating group of artists who are part of both the furniture design and the fine arts world. The gallery shop offers wonderful objects, prints, and multiples at great prices. I love that Kasmin put together an extraordinary retrospective exhibition of iconic pieces by Claude and François-Xavier Lalanne, the French furniture designers. Kasmin also represents Kenny Scharf, a living legend, and in 2011, hosted a show with 36 of Scharf's cosmic donuts.

James Cohan:
James and his wife Jane run this amazing gallery that represents some of the superstars of the contemporary art world, such as Beatriz Milhazes, Fred Tomaselli, and Yinka Shonibare, as well as such rising stars as Trenton Doyle Hancock and Simon Evans. Cohan is accessible and generous, as well as a pioneer of the Internet and the art world. In 2010, he founded and launched the VIP Art Fair, an internationally accessible online art fair that brings together some of the most prestigious galleries in the world for a few days under one cyber-roof.

Danziger Gallery:
Run by James Danziger, this gallery is a dream for lovers of photography. Danziger has a strong focus on fashion photography, a subject that is very relevant to my tastes and interests. The gallery represents Scott Schuman, the Sartorialist, and in 2010, showed the *Kate Moss Portfolio* curated by Kate Moss presenting a limited-edition series of 11 photographs of the model, shot by such masters such as Mario Testino, Chuck Close, and Bruce Weber.

Salon 94:
Salon 94 began operating as a gallery in the living room of Jeanne Greenberg Rohatyn's townhouse on East 94th Street and now includes two other spaces: one on the Bowery, near the New Museum, and one in Freeman Alley, also in the Lower East Side. I'm an admirer of the fluidity of their exhibitions and a raging fan of the artists they represent including Lorna Simpson, Laurie Simmons, and Marilyn Minter.

Eleven Rivington:
This small but already-expanding gallery carefully selects emerging or under-the-radar mid-career artists. It's good to check and see what up-and-coming talents it has spotted recently. On my personal radar: Chris Caccamise, Caetano de Almeida, and Valeska Soares.

The Hole:
This is one of my absolute favorite galleries. Kathy Grayson, its owner and founder, sharpened her eye while working with the legendary gallery owner, Jeffrey Deitch. She has taken the 4,000 square feet of the Hole, in SoHo, to another level. When she opened in 2011, Grayson exhibited the Miami collective FriendsWithYou and filled up the gallery with colorful, geometric dolls, including a giant, inflatable one. Theo Rosenblum, Joe Grillo, Evan Gruzis, Matt Stone, and Holton Rower are some of my favorites in this gallery.

Lumas:
This German gallery, with many international locations, is dedicated exclusively to photography. Since some of the best photographers in the world are German, and Lumas' curators are always on the lookout for the best undiscovered talent, the prints they bring from Germany to their other galleries are really extraordinary. From time to time, they release special editions of big names like Candida Höfer, Nan Goldin, and Juergen Teller.

Praxis Art:
Praxis represents a selection of mostly emerging, exceptional Latin American artists. Most of the artists share a talent for using bright colors and a unique execution of their media. From their roster, I'm very interested in the works of Brazilian artist Priscila de Carvalho and Colombian artist Alexis Duque.

WASHINGTON, D.C.

Industry Gallery:
Totally off the beaten path, as the main gallery is located in Washington, D.C., although it now has a sister gallery in Los Angeles, Craig Appelbaum has ventured into a kind of unchartered territory. He has opened a high-end gallery that is exclusively dedicated to showing the works of artists and furniture designers of the twenty-first century. Some of the highlights include the first solo show in the United States of Dutch artists Tejo Remy and René Veenhuizen, and the introduction of Tom Price, the famous British designer, to this side of the Atlantic.

PARIS

School Gallery:
Olivier Castaing, the handsome, charming Parisian who owns this gallery, is a fantastic collector, keeping most of his pieces in his apartment, located on the top floor of the gallery building, which is in a tiny alley in the Le Marais area. Among my favorites are Ghyslain Bertholon, Yveline Tropea, and Julio Villani.

Galerie 208:
Located at the very end of the Boulevard St.-Germain, Galerie 208 is a gallery that makes itself accessible by presenting artists who explore current social and political topics—younger and mid-career talents such as Michel Soubeyran, Davide Nido, and Tony Vasquez. I also love that the gallery puts together sculpture shows or large installations *hors les murs,* or outside the walls, in public spaces.

Galerie Perrotin:
Emmanuel Perrotin likes to take risks and that makes his shows and choice of artists a lot cooler than other galleries. Most of his artists share an element of wit and satire. They include conceptualists like Maurizio Cattelan and Elmgreen & Dragset, as well as street artist Kaws. Takashi Murakami, the "superflat" artist, a term that encompasses the use of a wide variety of media, from painting to animation, and that mixes high and low in the context of Japan's pop cultural society, is one of the gallery's stars. Perrotin also has a shop that offers prints and editions at a fraction of what some of the works in the gallery cost, *bien sur.*

Galerie Envie d'art:
Cathy and Yann Bombard run this gallery, which occupies three different spaces in Paris. I love the easy going feel of the artists they represent and the happiness that surrounds most of their shows. Their prices, too, are irresistible. Sometimes feeling good and falling aesthetically in love with the art you see is all you really need. From their stable of artists, Corinne Dalle-Ore, Nicolas Pichon, and Luigi Visconti are my stand-outs.

Galerie Eva Hober:
This gallery is located on a hidden street in Le Marais, and most of the artists it represents share an element of macabre fantasy, blurring the line between the grotesque and the fantastic. Although most of what the gallery shows can be filtered through the eyes of a cynical New Yorker or Parisian, or someone who is not easily offended, this gallery is not for the uninitiated. My absolute favorites are Jérôme Zonder, Myriam Mechita, Gregory Forstner, and Maike Freess.

Galerie Kreo:
Located two blocks from the Boulevard Saint-Germain and two blocks from the Pont Neuf, Galerie Kreo is a magic space for contemporary designers who play with furniture and object designs, ranging from sofas, to rugs, to lamps. The Krzentowskis are a couple that is committed to finding the most innovative pieces and to giving free rein to the artists and designers they represent. Pierre Charpin and Marc Newson are, in my opinion, Kreo's best.

LONDON

Lazarides Gallery:
Steve Lazarides is a genius. He is quite invested in the world of street art. He was the one who legitimately represented the artist Banksy for the first time and put together his first solo shows in Los Angeles and London. (After a professional relationship of almost ten years, they no longer work together.) Like most street-art lovers, Lazarides thrives when he is pushing boundaries. The gallery has two spaces in London and one in Newcastle. My favorite artists at the gallery are FAILE, Bast, Blu, and Nina Pandolfo.

White Cube:
It's very hard to talk about contemporary art galleries in London without mentioning White Cube. This gallery has earned a spot as one of the most influential in the contemporary art world since Jay Joplin opened it in 1993. What started as a white cube—a room on the second floor of a small building on Duke Street—is today spread out over three spaces of more than 60,000 square feet. Some of the Young British Artists (YBA) like Gary Hume and Marc Quinn are part of White Cube's stable, as is the genius German photographer Andreas Gursky.

Victoria Miro:
Victoria is a Grande Dame of Contemporary Art in England. She treats everyone with great respect and zealously manages the careers of her talented artists, such as Chris Ofili, Yayoi Kusama, Maria Nepomuceno, and the estate of Francesca Woodman.

Paradise Row:
A fun, cutting-edge gallery that represents emerging artists and mid-career talents like Diann Bauer, Martha Colburn, and Margarita Gluzberg.

AROUND THE WORLD

Gagosian:
Larry Gagosian has built an empire of high-end galleries across the hemispheres that includes the cities of New York, Rome, Athens, Moscow, Los Angeles, Geneva, Hong Kong, London, and Paris, and for that alone, he deserves my respect. Gagosian and his team, composed mostly of fantastic women or "Gagosiènnes," select some of the best talents in the world. Gagosian is also truly impressive in his ability to put together shows of such modern masters as Pablo Picasso, Diego Giacometti, and Claude Monet that would make any museum exhibit look incomplete by comparison. Of the mid-career group of artists that Gagosian represents, Adam McEwen and Anselm Reyle are currently holding my attention.

For addresses and websites, see page 152.

OPPOSITE A sculptural mobile installation of metal and mixed-media by Brazilian artist Beatriz Milhazes was hung in the James Cohan Gallery in New York in 2009. Called *Gamboa*, it was created by Milhazes to be exhibited at Prospect.1 New Orleans, a biennial multi-venue of contemporary art.

VIK MUNIZ is an extraordinary Brazilian artist who holds a hard-earned spot as one of the most important contemporary artists of our time. Muniz is very prolific and an incredible human being. When I saw his work for the first time, I realized I had to own one of his pieces. I was captivated by its originality, uniqueness, as well as the beauty and passion in the work. I immediately became a fan, a follower, and a collector. Muniz works mostly in photography and each of his series usually consists of six images and an artist's proof, produced in two sizes. The subject matter of Muniz's work is compelling, and the story behind the photographs is as interesting as the images themselves. For example, Muniz will reproduce a photograph of a child roaming the streets of São Paulo using urban waste left over from the carnival. Inspired by an old master work—*Sunflowers* by Vincent Van Gogh or Caravaggio's *Medusa*—he creates an alternative setting with pigments, diamonds, caviar, tiny pieces of paper, junk, chocolate syrup, or toys, as in my favorite series entitled *Rebus.* Muniz puts it all together in his studios, in Brooklyn, New York, or Rio de Janeiro, and photographs the compositions with a special camera and lens, sometimes from a considerable height. His technique is flawless, and his images are colorful, vivid, and absolutely beautiful. His assistants work hard making sure that the end product delivered to collectors, galleries, and museums is impeccable.

TOP I was so impressed when I entered the exhibition *Pictures of Magazines 2* at the Sikkema Jenkins gallery in New York in the fall of 2011. This collage series had a quantity of texture and detail that was so spectacular that I invited many of my clients and friends to see the show. *La Bacchante (after Gustave Courbet)* was one of the artworks that I advised a client of mine to buy. She did.

ABOVE In New York in the fall of 2010, I was photographed with Vik Muniz at the premiere of his documentary *Waste Land,* which was nominated for an Oscar in 2011.

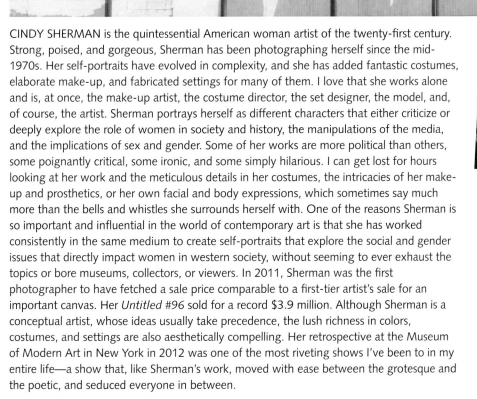

CINDY SHERMAN is the quintessential American woman artist of the twenty-first century. Strong, poised, and gorgeous, Sherman has been photographing herself since the mid-1970s. Her self-portraits have evolved in complexity, and she has added fantastic costumes, elaborate make-up, and fabricated settings for many of them. I love that she works alone and is, at once, the make-up artist, the costume director, the set designer, the model, and, of course, the artist. Sherman portrays herself as different characters that either criticize or deeply explore the role of women in society and history, the manipulations of the media, and the implications of sex and gender. Some of her works are more political than others, some poignantly critical, some ironic, and some simply hilarious. I can get lost for hours looking at her work and the meticulous details in her costumes, the intricacies of her make-up and prosthetics, or her own facial and body expressions, which sometimes say much more than the bells and whistles she surrounds herself with. One of the reasons Sherman is so important and influential in the world of contemporary art is that she has worked consistently in the same medium to create self-portraits that explore the social and gender issues that directly impact women in western society, without seeming to ever exhaust the topics or bore museums, collectors, or viewers. In 2011, Sherman was the first photographer to have fetched a sale price comparable to a first-tier artist's sale for an important canvas. Her *Untitled #96* sold for a record $3.9 million. Although Sherman is a conceptual artist, whose ideas usually take precedence, the lush richness in colors, costumes, and settings are also aesthetically compelling. Her retrospective at the Museum of Modern Art in New York in 2012 was one of the most riveting shows I've been to in my entire life—a show that, like Sherman's work, moved with ease between the grotesque and the poetic, and seduced everyone in between.

TOP In 2012, several buildings on busy streets in New York were plastered with billboards of Cindy Sherman's self-portraits. This one, on Houston Street near Sixth Avenue, showed her 2008 *Untitled #465*.

ABOVE Cindy Sherman and I were captured on the opening night of her incredible retrospective at the Museum of Modern Art. She is every bit as fascinating and fashion-driven as anyone who has seen her work can imagine.

TRACEY EMIN is part contemporary art royalty and part rock star. She has gone with her art to places where a lot of people don't want to, baring her soul and willing to share intimate details of her private life, without being a bit ashamed. Emin's drawings and monoprints—raw, exceptional, and far from perfect—convey a story that is in the making, things that are happening or that could have happened to any of us. She is a consummate storyteller. I'm drawn to the intensity in her work and her life. She took neon art and signage to the next level by engaging the viewer, sometimes with two words, sometimes with entire phrases. Emin devises exquisite embroideries and patchwork quilts, covered with poignant messages, such as "I Want an International Lover that Loves me More than the World." So brilliant. Emin is also a fantastic writer, and her weekly articles in the London newspaper, *The Independent*, were compiled into an amusing book called *My Life in a Column*. What I love the most about Emin is her honesty and her strong spirit, which surface in all her work. That's the degree of emotion that most artists should convey. She is truly one of a kind.

ABOVE Tracey Emin is one of the funniest people I have ever met. Her self-deprecating sense of humor and her unabashed personality fascinate me.

LEFT Emin's show *Only God Knows I'm Good* was exhibited at Lehmann Maupin, the gallery that represents her in New York, in December 2009.

FLAVIA DA RIN is one of the most promising South American talents. She is an artist who produces photographic self-portraits nearly exclusively, manipulating the images either to portray herself in a fairy tale, circus, or joke—or sometimes as a bald-headed boy, or a fancy socialite sporting a Hermès bag. Da Rin, who is from Argentina, has told me that her creative process is fueled by other disciplines and by people who can easily navigate other worlds, like those of fashion or industrial design. She has collaborated twice with Hermès to design the store windows in her native Buenos Aires, and in Singapore, where a dazzling show, entitled *Discovery & Journey*, accompanied the window display. In 2007, Da Rin created the images used by Cartier to re-launch their *Love* jewelry collection under the premise "How far would you go for LOVE?" A consistent and committed artist, her work has been exhibited in all the major contemporary art museums in Argentina, and she has been selected by a worldwide team of renowned curators as one of the top young contemporary artists in the world, as reflected in the "Younger than Jesus" survey that was assembled during New York's New Museum Triennial research phase.

PREVIOUS PAGES The Hermès Foundation has committed a lot of resources to encourage young, as well as established, artists to showcase their talents in collaboration with their brand. Flavia Da Rin, one of my favorite Latin American artists, designed the windows for the Maison Hermès in Singapore in 2008, using her characteristic self-portrait photographs, which in this case are equally reminiscent of fairies by the Italian Renaissance master Sandro Botticelli as the work of contemporary American artist John Currin.

CHRISTA JOO HYUN D'ANGELO exemplifies the globalization of the world: Her parents are of Italian descent, she was born in Korea, grew up in New York, studied in Baltimore, Maryland, and Krakow, Poland, and is now based in Berlin, Germany. Since I discovered her work at the Volta Art Fair in New York in 2012, I have been following her development. Her work explores a topic that really interests me: Our society's voracity for visual content and consumerism, particularly in the areas of fashion and celebrity. In her body of work, I have been especially fascinated by her cut-out book sculptures, her wallpapers, and her very colorful and sensual fashion-inspired collages. I expect to see her doing more in the future. D'Angelo is tiny and has an infectious laugh. Like a true New Yorker, she is sweet and tough at the same time and also smart as a whip. Although she loves living in Berlin, New York will always be her home. Both cities, she said, are "intrinsically real in the sense that you cannot easily shadow the grittier robust aspects of life on the street. People voice themselves and don't seem to censor or at least tolerate censorship." I totally agree.

LEFT Christa Joo Hyun D'Angelo's solo installation at the Volta Art Fair in New York in the spring of 2012 included wallpaper with the face of a half-mutilated Linda Evangelista that has been replaced with the picture of a white cat, which she wittily entitled *Cat Woman*. It captured my attention to the extent that I ended up buying the only neon sculpture she had made to date, and even became friends with her.

CORINNE DALLE-ORE is a neo-pop artist from St. Tropez in the south of France, who lives in Paris, and adores New York. I bought one of her most striking pieces many years ago. I fell in love with Dalle-Ore's way of recreating old and new characters, luminaries, and movie stars. She is as delightful and beautiful as her work. Visiting her in her Paris studio felt almost like visiting an old friend. Besides her warmth and great sense of humor, the pieces hanging on the walls felt so familiar and provided a kind of safe space where I felt really embraced. I love her Andy Warhol-inspired idea of making everyday objects, as well as photographs of cities and celebrities, much more interesting, appealing, and colorful than they often really are.

LEFT Dalle-Ore is authentic and real, and visiting her studio in Paris seemed just natural after so many years of admiring her work.

OPPOSITE Like me, Dalle-Ore is a great fan of Frida Kahlo's, and has been inspired by her life and career. The mixed-media canvas that now hangs in my living room depicts a black-and-white photograph of the iconic artist with a bright tangerine background, flowers, and raw phrases in Spanish.

FAILE is a Brooklyn, New York-based street art collective made up of Patrick McNeil and Patrick Miller. I remember when I first moved to New York in 2000 and saw some of the walls in the East Village wheat-pasted with FAILE's infamous girl and bunny, a design that shifts ambiguously between the erotic and the childish. I thought: *Wow! What a smart way to express two aspects that can be at times so vague and yet so powerful in any adult's life.* I love their mix of street art and high aesthetics, subliminal messages, and well-thought-out design. I'm quite a fan of FAILE and the Patricks: Not only are they incredible artists who are unafraid to work with a lot of different media—including wooden boxes and prayer wheels—but they are also helpful, committed, and have allowed me to visit their studio many times! I love their use of imagery because it represents so many aspects of our daily life: consumerism, political statements, jokes, and criticisms of extreme capitalism, fashion, sex, and references to Americana, all blended masterfully in collages, wood pieces, reliefs, prints, and canvases. Their shows are mind-blowing, either in a gallery setting such as that of Perry Rubenstein, a dealer formerly based in New York but who is now in Los Angeles, at Lazarides in London, or in museums, such as the sensational *Street Art* show at the Tate Modern in London in 2008, where one of their pieces was a massive 240-square-foot collage that was affixed to the Tate's exterior and was admired by curators, collectors, and critics.

THESE PAGES Visiting the FAILE studio in Brooklyn, New York, is a treat. It is full of surprises, and there is always an aura of mystery. Patrick McNeil and Patrick Miller don't like to be overexposed and don't always like to have visitors, so I'm grateful for their generosity. Their cavernous building is full of enormous rooms distributed over two large floors filled top to bottom with incredible pieces of their own art as well as works they have collected from other street artists who are their friends.

AVAF's vibrant and original art enthralls me. Everything this collective puts out is visually mesmerizing, while retaining a deeper layer of meaning. Eli Sudbrack, the Brazilian half of AVAF, is warm and loving. In 2003, I went to a show in the now-closed Deitch Projects gallery in Manhattan's SoHo area. The artists went by the name of Assume Vivid Astro Focus or AVAF, a Brazilian-French collective duo formed by the extraordinary Sudbrack, who, like my husband, is from Rio de Janeiro, and Christophe Hamaide-Pierson, a Frenchman. I could not believe my eyes when I set foot in that show! The most amazing wallpaper, which included a rainbow collage of dazzling colors, tapestry-like designs, people who seemed to be taken out of the Rio carnival parade, extraordinary abstract shapes and flowers, inspirations from Rock 'n' Roll and samba music, and an image of a man posing naked from the waist up sporting a cross around his neck—who, I later learned, was a famous Russian X-rated film star—covered the walls, ceilings, and floors in a psychedelic yet coherent way that engaged everyone who attended that hot summer show. Live Brazilian music was blasting and people in costumes and masks were dancing and singing. The uniqueness and boldness of it all made me an AVAF fan immediately, and years later, also a collector. I can't get tired of AVAF's works and I'm always in awe of their creativity and imagination. Being Latin, I'm drawn to their carnival-like prints, explosive colors, and in-your-face interactions with the spectators. I am deeply connected to their bold aesthetics and profound themes, which deal with gender, race, identity, and sometimes, pure happiness and *joie de vivre*. They have been a great inspiration for me. Sudbrack and Hamaide-Pierson have explored a variety of topics including masks, carnival, gender roles and sexuality, and most specifically, transvestites. In a series of drawings entitled *Cyclopes Trannies*, they showed the exaggerated features, big lips,

glossy eyes, and giant lashes of post-operations subjects. AVAF has done some interesting collaborations with the fashion brands Comme des Garçons, Le Sportsac, and Melissa Shoes—for which the artists not only designed special edition flip-flops, but also an installation with large neon sculptures. That 5,500-square-foot pop-up workshop, designed in collaboration with Lady Gaga and Nicola Formichetti, her stylist and creative director, which opened at Barneys department store in New York in December 2011, was a huge success. Hundreds of products—from holiday tree ornaments to leather clothing—were displayed in what Sudbrack called "a very immersive space where people could have an art experience," like visiting a museum or gallery. What I love about artists like AVAF is that they never compromise and they always do their best and boldest, either in a massive, albeit luxurious, store, at the 2004 Whitney Museum Biennial in New York, or in their 2005 show at the more modest Tate Liverpool in England.

OPPOSITE The AVAF studio in Williamsburg, Brooklyn, is full of objects from which Eli Sudbrack gets inspiration, including Pucci prints, Gaetano Pesce vases, and interesting masks. No wonder I love AVAF art so much.

ABOVE After many years of my being a fan and a collector, and placing AVAF works on many of my clients' walls, Eli Sudbrack invited me to hang out in his fascinating Brooklyn studio. While I was there, he took my large AVAF monograph and drew a tranny inside the book, just for me!

MINT & SERF consists of Mikhail Sokovikov, known as Mint, and Jason Aaron Wall, or Serf, my unruly Rock 'n' Roll graffiti friends, who, since 1997, have made the streets of New York their canvas. What I like about these guys is their dedication to be truthful to who they are and to express that through their art. What began as quasi-vandalism, with several encounters with the New York Police Department, has turned into raw but complex compositions of graffiti traces, acrylic tables, and light boxes where spray-paint cans are masterfully displayed. The fashion designer Marc Jacobs commissioned one of their taggings for the windows of one of his boutiques on Bleecker Street, in New York's West Village. They also took on the project to curate the art collection of the super-trendy Ace Hotel, on West 29th Street in Manhattan, while also painting murals in several of the rooms, and they got an invitation from the band Metallica to paint the walls of the Metallica Museum during an epic two-day music festival in New Jersey in 2012. I collaborated with Mint & Serf as part of an art series I put together at SoHo House, a club in the meatpacking district of New York. To my absolute delight, the event jumpstarted other opportunities for them, including some wildly successful ones where they were commissioned to paint amazing graffiti pieces on the club's roof deck, where revelers hung out drinking cocktails on hot summer nights.

THESE PAGES Mint & Serf's fantastic studio in TriBeCa has an enormous skylight and walls covered with giant-sized spray-painted canvases. I was thrilled to see a lot of their different pieces in one place—from bronze and heavy plaster reliefs in neon colors, with their trademark "MIRF" symbol, to plaques and silkscreens with cynical messages related to the state of the economy. Spending time with them at their studio is like getting a reality check, but a very artistic one.

GAETANO PESCE is a legend, a creative genius, and a visionary ahead of his time. When my friend Craig Appelbaum told me that the Italian designer had invited me to visit his studio, I was elated. I have been collecting some of his pieces for years and have also placed many in my clients' apartments. A consummate architect, designer, and artist, Pesce has made New York his home since 1980. He has been creating extraordinary buildings, chairs, sofas, vases, jewelry, accessories, shoes, and anything that he can dream of, since the 1960s, always with great success, and with the acclaim of the press and critics. His huge studio is in a loft in Manhattan's SoHo. The place is a feast for the eyes, with strong saturated-color objects made of resin, foam, a jelly-like plastic, wood, and metal. His prototypes of tables and chairs are all over the place, as are his jewelry pieces. Of course, that day, I wore one of my Pesce rings. Pesce is funny, sharp, and quick when answering questions and recalling facts and details. I told him that one of my favorite pieces of all time is his *La Mamma* chair, designed for B&B Italia in 1969. He explained what was behind its creation: The lounge chair is shaped like a female body and refers to the objectification of women in an era of sex bunnies and silicone-filled breasts. Pesce took the design even further by attaching a round ottoman to the chair with a chain, illustrating the objectified woman as a prisoner. How smart is that?

THESE PAGES When I visited Gaetano Pesce in his studio, we talked for hours and I felt quite lucky to have accessed his world. In the end, I left with the sensation of having had quite a memorable day visiting an iconic master.

STREET ART AND THE REBEL IN ME

Graffiti, the unsolicited marking of public property, has been around for centuries. The 1960s, however, were important for graffiti and street art, particularly in New York. Washington Heights seems to be where the movement, as we know it, really started. At the time, street artists began using nicknames and/or symbols to mark public property and their work. This phenomenon was called "tagging." Keith Haring, for example, who is now so famous, tagged a lot of subway cars and walls with his most often-used symbol, the Radiant Baby. The 1970s and 1980s saw the consolidation of street art and graffiti. Jean-Michel Basquiat—one of my absolute favorite artists—Haring, Futura (2000), Blade, Crash, Lady Pink, and many of the most famous graffiti artists in the world started tagging walls in that sketchy New York of the 1970s. All of these artists ended up transitioning from the streets to galleries and museums by being invited to exhibit their work around the world in respected settings they had never dreamed of. The evolution of both graffiti and street art has resulted in a much more elaborate and technical form of art, not only in New York, but internationally. In the inner circles, where street culture converges with the art world, graffiti is viewed as a separate form of art. It is usually linked to vandalism and clandestine spray-paint cans, whereas street art is considered a more refined movement that has crawled its way up into galleries. Street art is mostly expressed in a beautified and more calculated way, through the use of stencils and wheat pasting. Graffiti, on the other hand, is raw and visceral. To me, the most fascinating part of both movements is the culture behind them. The fact that the artists are inspired by large metropoli, with enormous buildings, busy streets, and interesting people, as well as social, political, and economic issues, is all related to what daily life has become in big cities. I grew up in a crazy, chaotic city where all the walls were marked with graffiti, and now, as an adult, having spent so many years living in New York where graffiti and street art seem to be intertwined in its own cultural history, it's impossible for me not to be seduced by it. Among my favorite graffiti and street artists are: Miss Van, who is French and now lives in Barcelona, FAILE, Os Gêmeos, Banksy and Nick Walker in London, Barry McGee from San Francisco, Kenny Scharf from Los Angeles, Mint & Serf, and Kaws in New York. I have had the good fortune of meeting and working with many of these artists, as well as observing their creative processes, sometimes even from inside their studios. While an original piece created by any of these artists can be worth several thousand dollars

now, all of them have released excellent limited-edition prints and objects that can be purchased for a few hundred dollars and can enhance any space. Not just because these multiples are usually vibrant and colorful, but also because their messages range from playful to political to sarcastic, it's hard not to be amused or deeply engaged by them. In many of my projects, one way or another, there is a reference to street art. I believe one of the coolest things about graffiti and street artists is that they never stop tagging. They love working outdoors, whether on commissioned or illegal work. At least in New York, however, unsolicited graffiti in public or private property is against the law. I'm also fascinated by how emotional this art is. If there's a form of art that is unadulterated and free of constraints, it is graffiti and street art.

The art market is hot in this area because of the number of artists who are being represented in galleries and have been invited by major museums to participate in group shows. In addition, street art has made its way to auction houses. Since I am so much into street art, I suggest that my clients pay close attention to the evolution and transition periods of artists who go from tagging walls to museum exhibitions. They usually become highly sought after, and prices for their work soar astronomically. For example, Basquiat's extraordinary paintings are nowadays rarely even available in the marketplace, and when they are, they are immediately put up at auction with prices in the millions of dollars. But we don't have to go that far back in time. I know a couple who bought a Banksy piece in 2004 for under $5,000. The same piece today has been appraised at more than $100,000. For my list of top street-art galleries, see page 152.

LEFT, FROM TOP Fantastic street art covers the doors of this garage in the El Born district in Barcelona, across the street from the famous restaurant, Commerce 24; the large mural in Melbourne, Australia, is full of interesting details and friendly creatures; and the El Raval neighborhood, in Barcelona, has some of the best street art I have seen. This door was painted by the French artist, Miss Van.

OPPOSITE In June of 2012, the British artist known as Banksy was thought to have graffiti'ed the image of a young boy sewing the Union Jack bunting in preparation for Queen Elizabeth II's Diamond Jubilee on the wall of a store in Wood Green, North London. The piece is also a reference to how kids in Asia and South America have to work to satisfy the Western world of consumption.

TOP I have been a fan since 2008, when the Brazilian artists Os Gêmeos took over the corner of Houston Street and the Bowery, a New York site for the best street art.

ABOVE Gustavo and Otavio Pandolfo of Os Gêmeos and I were photographed in the yard of Manhattan's P.S. 11.

OPPOSITE The 50-foot-tall mural commissioned by the City of New York for P.S. 11 is really a gift to the children, and those of us who live in Chelsea get to see it almost every day. The boy wears shorts with the flags of many countries, and, missing a shoe, recalls the children living in the *favelas*, or slums, of Brazil.

OS GÊMEOS, the twins in Portuguese, are Otavio and Gustavo Pandolfo from São Paulo. For a long time, I have been obsessed with two things: Graffiti and contemporary Brazilian artists. So, it was a marriage made in heaven when I was able to meet the identical twin brothers. I had been following these guys for a long time, who, for two decades, have been painting together and expressing themselves through the coolest art. They started as graphic designers, but when they met American artist Barry McGee in Brazil around 1993, their lives changed, and so did their art. Today, they have earned their place as part of the Brazilian royalty of contemporary art, and are also some of the most important artists in the world. Their work has been shown at the Havana Biennial in Cuba, the Tate Modern in London, the Museum of Contemporary Art in Tokyo, the Museum Het Domein Sittard in the Netherlands, the Museum of Contemporary Art in San Diego, and The Saatchi Gallery in London. It took me a long time to be able to get one of their pieces for my collection, and when I did, I gave it the honorable place that it deserves in my living room. It came from Italy after lots of negotiations with the dealer, and I could not be happier or more thrilled with it. I really enjoyed meeting the twins and hanging out while watching their progress painting a mural that occupies the entire west façade of P.S. 11, a six-story public school in the Chelsea area of New York. Working really hard and standing at considerable heights on top of giant cranes in the harsh heat, it took them about a week to get a mural of that size completed. Os Gêmeos' murals, pieces, and installations are always deeply influenced by their Brazilian roots—the folklore, the politics, and the economic disparities of their native country. But these artists are also imaginative and playful, constantly referring to a secret place in their shared dreams, a magical and sometimes sad place called *Tritrez*. It's no wonder that the names of some of their exhibitions sound so ethereal: *Too Far Too Close*; *Pra quem mora lá, o céu é lá*, which loosely translates to *For Those who Live There, Heaven is There*; or *Nos Braços de um Anjo,* which means *In the Arms of an Angel.*

KENNY SCHARF, the American artist, is the king of Pop Surrealism, a term he coined in 1981. He was artist Keith Haring's roommate, one of Jean-Michel Basquiat's closest friends, and a dear pal and admirer of Andy Warhol. Scharf is as talented an artist as he is generous and good-looking. I have always been enthralled by his ability to turn mundane objects into fantastic things through his art. Nothing is off-limits to him, and everything can become something else. He is from California, has a home in New York, and another in Bahia, Brazil. All of them are chock full of fantastic trinkets, most of which he has created himself. Nick Olney, director of the Paul Kasmin Gallery in New York, graciously arranged my visit to Scharf's studio, and all I could say was "Wow!" We all had such a fantastic time in his basement, which he transformed years ago into a Cosmic Cavern, with painted floors, neon lights, plastic ornaments, toys, objects, and glow-in-the-dark painted chairs, furniture, and walls. This space is where Scharf throws parties that are reminiscent of the golden era of the 1980s. Many of the objects left in the studio, some for more than 20 years, from wigs to whistles, have become part of the permanent installation. Scharf has influenced many artists, including Dearraindrop and Joe Grillo, as well as AVAF. We talked about the 1980s and about the influence of that time on today, about how his oldest daughter, Zena, was the inspiration for Haring's famous Radiant Baby image, and how Tereza, the mother of his daughters, inspired Haring when she was pregnant. It's very exciting for me to hear Scharf talk about those legends of the streets of New York—who are no longer around. He also told me that Haring, if he were still alive, would have been thrilled to have been featured in this book—one of the best compliments I have ever received. I left Scharf's studio feeling quite buzzed and optimistic.

THESE PAGES In Kenny Scharf's studio, many other artists' works also hang on the walls—a testament to his inclusive spirit and open-mindedness. I posed with Nick Olney, *top right*, and Scharf during my visit to the studio.

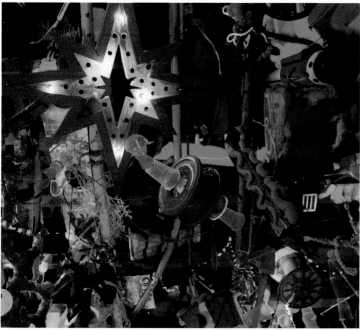

LIVING WITH ART

In the past ten to fifteen years, for a variety of reasons, contemporary art has become the hottest thing. One explanation is that, at some point, good collectors couldn't get their hands on top Impressionist or modern art pieces because of the high prices the available works were fetching, and because of the scarcity of pieces from these periods, most of which had been either bought by or donated to museums, or had already been acquired by collectors. Also, people now feel that it's cool and fun to have the stuff of their own time, as it represents who they are and expresses the shared sentiments of today. I'm a collector who totally subscribes to this last reason for collecting contemporary art. I connect with the passion of living artists, and I love to have them in my home. Contemporary art is usually very versatile when placed in someone's home—although true collectors don't buy art thinking about where they will hang a particular piece—but it makes no sense to have a warehouse or art-storage facility full of works that are not being appreciated. Contemporary art can be mixed with more traditional pieces, creating the tension that I love and for which I'm known as a designer, or it can also be put together with very sleek and minimalist furniture to create a gallery-like vibe, in which the art takes over the room. Aside from questions of personal taste, people are generally afraid of buying art that pushes the envelope. Sometimes people tend to spend too much time looking at the same staged rooms in the catalogs they receive from furniture chain stores to make choices when buying art. Having one's own collection and living with art is an extraordinary opportunity for people to express themselves in ways that they may not otherwise be able to. When it comes to the size of a piece of contemporary art, judging by the number of auction houses and gallery shows that display and sell large pieces, bigger is usually better. Although not a hard and fast rule, displaying a large-scale piece of art is actually one of the most amazing ways to transform the entire look of a room in a way that feels both aesthetically compelling and smart. I'm not at all opposed to smaller works, in particular when they can be displayed as in a gallery, or when wall space is limited. Smaller works are inviting and intriguing, and force people to look closer and be more aware of details. People tend to hang their art either too high or too low on the wall. As a rule of thumb, a large piece should be placed eight to ten inches away from the piece of furniture directly beneath it. But it is very difficult to have just one rule to determine placement, since the space as a

whole must be taken into account. Often, larger works call for lower positioning, while smaller ones can be hung higher. Another common mistake is to display pieces in places where they could be damaged by direct sunlight. Acrylics, oils, and charcoals on canvas can be harmed, but watercolors and photographs are especially sensitive. This is a particularly challenging and recurring situation in many New York apartments. People also tend to hesitate placing artworks of different techniques—such as acrylics on canvas, photographs, and sculpture—in the same room. This is very different from mixing pieces together from different movements and periods of time that might not relate to each other and which I don't like. And when contemporary art is displayed at home, rooms don't have to be minimal or plain. Integrating contemporary art with different styles of furniture and accessories is one of the ways to give a room depth and to create the most interesting and talked-about interiors.

LEFT, FROM TOP Two wood panels, by French artist Nicolas Pichon, fit perfectly in this hallway; wood sculptures by Frankfort, Kentucky-based artist L.A. Watson sit on top a bookshelf; a large abstract oil-on-canvas piece by San Francisco-based artist David Hewitt contrasts beautifully with the vintage dining table; and two graphic canvases by New York artist Peter Tunney enliven a living room.

OPPOSITE Arranging small pieces in a gallery-like vignette usually generates visual impact and avoids the dilution that may occur if each were to be displayed on its own. In this grouping, *clockwise from the top*, are a silkscreen by Os Gêmeos, a limited-edition print by the Assume Vivid Astro Focus, a print-collage by Mickalene Thomas, a black-and-white photograph by Pamela Hanson, a metal print by Corinne Dalle-Ore, and a collage on canvas by Joe Grillo.

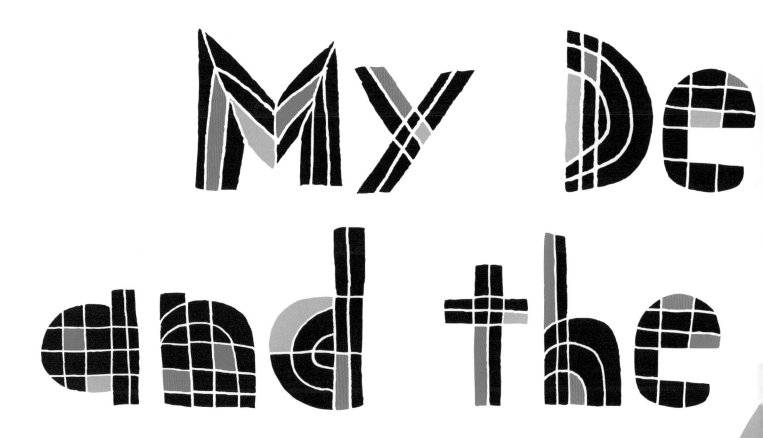

signs Art ving

Choosing Compelling Photographs

Nothing gets New Yorkers more excited than extraordinary views of Manhattan. The feeling of seeing an unobstructed panorama from a very high floor is like being on top of the world. When I visited this apartment in TriBeCa for the first time, it was completely empty, so I had no choice but to fall in love with the views. I immediately told my client that he needed to forgo curtains and shades on behalf of the sexy sights of lower Manhattan and the Hudson River. My challenge with this project was that I had only four weeks to complete it—from the design phase to installation. A deadline that, I'm happy to report, I met. My client wanted a homey yet masculine scheme that was restrained but not sterile. I decided on using greys and blues for the main palette, as they are subdued. Although not usually my first choices for a color scheme—I'm usually inclined to go for hotter hues—I knew that I could take the interiors of this apartment to the next level by adding bold photography to the walls, so I curated an art collection composed mostly of compelling photographs. I thought about the sensibility of my client, and I was able to assemble a balanced selection that ranged from dramatic, visually profound architectural images, such as one of the Opera House in Wiesbaden, Germany, by the German artist Rafael Neff, to the edgy and theatrical shot of a model by the Canadian-born Benjamin Kanarek. I also added playful elements that I knew were going to warm up the interior and give it a sense of humor, without compromising the feeling of being in a grown-up apartment, such as a blue-and-white chess set for the office, and dramatic and amusing Renaissance-style plates on the kitchen wall. The overall result was exactly what we had envisioned: an apartment that is not only calm and elegant, and really feels like home, but one that is sophisticated, and where the artworks function as great conversation pieces.

ABOVE When we photographed this apartment, I asked the super-talented photographer, Scott Jones, to take my picture at the very end of the day. I rolled the Eames chair from the office and it took only one click of the camera. I was really happy that the photo shoot had gone so well, and it gave me an excuse for a new portrait.

OPPOSITE ABOVE I was not at all intimidated about designing the empty space, curating an art collection, and having all the furnishings installed in under four weeks.

OPPOSITE This is how the living room looked after I sprinkled some fairy dust over it. The client loved leather, so to please him, I ordered a coffee-colored leather sofa. Above it, I placed an acrylic-mounted photograph by Rafael Neff. I love the drama and intensity of architectural shots. Neff is influenced by the Düsseldorf school of photography, and at times, some of his work reminds me of the oeuvre of Candida Höfer, one of the most important artists in the school. In the foyer, I hung a chandelier made of capiz shells from the Philippines that is discreet yet creates an interesting statement. The console, mirror, and bust are all antiques.

PREVIOUS PAGES In the living room, I loved that I had a chance to work with colors like blue and grey, which I don't usually use. The rug is by Thomas Paul, a New York designer who started out in fashion and then transitioned to home design, the blue sofa in the back is from Blu Dot, and the antique French chairs were paired with pillows made from Turkish ikats. I found a very cool edition of images by the New York-based artist Marc Dennis from Artspace.com to place between the windows. The piece is called *Honey Bunny* and is a hyper-realistic still life that depicts a handgun, a string of pearls, fragments of lingerie, and a little bunny that makes reference to one of American artist Jeff Koons' most famous images. The dining area is furnished with a Knoll Pedestal table, chairs by the Finnish architect Eero Saarinen and an Arco lamp by Italian designers Achille Castiglioni and Pier Giacomo Castiglioni. To keep a playful mood, I used games as accessories, positioning a vintage croquet set under an assemblage of vintage toy pieces by New York artist Elizabeth Rosen. A set of blocks that depict the history of the American Presidents, and ceramic marbles depicting all the letters of the alphabet, are displayed on the coffee tables.

LEFT I have used the series of versatile melamine plates, from the British company Whitbread Wilkinson in partnership with the National Gallery in London, in different ways in a few of my projects. The plates, which depict details from paintings by Italian masters, also make great gifts. Andrea Solario's *Giovanni Cristoforo Longoni*, Paris Bordone's *Portrait of Young Woman*, and Antonello da Messina's *Portrait of a Man* all stare intently from the wall in the kitchen.

OPPOSITE The kitchen has a wonderful view of downtown Manhattan. Located on the 50th floor, the apartment has the most inspiring vistas from every window. Obstructing them in any way would have been a crime.

LEFT The guest bedroom doubles as a home office. As the client likes vintage photography, I found him a set of 1940s black-and-white images of downtown Manhattan by the German-American photographer Andreas Lyonel Feininger. The standing tripod lamp is by Authentic Models, a Dutch company, and the rug was designed by Spanish designer Sandra Figuerola for Gandía Blasco. The vintage Mexican chess set on the desk contributes to the light-hearted feeling of the room.

BELOW LEFT In continuing to curate a strong photography collection, I added two pieces of similar size and color to the master bedroom. The one on the left is by the German photographer Joerg Maxzin, and the woman in the red dress is by Erin Cone, a Texan artist who now lives in Santa Fe, New Mexico.

OPPOSITE Canadian fashion photographer Benjamin Kanarek, who has shot many editorial features and covers for such magazines as *Vogue Paris*, *Elle Spain*, and *Madame Figaro*, has also created beautiful pieces of fine art. He has captivated me with his erotic subjects and moody backgrounds. This work makes a very sexy statement in the dining area—it's very unexpected, and I love it because of that.

Ethnic Influences

The first time I entered this apartment, three things struck me: The purity of the light; the sensation of not being in a city, as all I could see outside were treetops; and that the owner had a lot of books. My client, a born and bred New Yorker, told me that she loved the beach, had traveled extensively, and was particularly drawn to South America, Africa, and Asia. I translated that information into my design, turning her apartment into a happy place with a palette of blues, greens, and oranges. I put together a collection of African dolls from South Africa, Ghana, Tanzania, and Namibia, found one-of-a-kind pieces of furniture, bought fine photography, and commissioned prints and editions that reflected her passions. I also added accessories—German pottery from the 1950s, vintage acrylic trays, and Josef Frank fabric-covered pillows that I combined with more contemporary furniture, such as the Blu Dot bookcase, red Real Good Chairs, and an orange sectional by the California-born designer Edgar Blazona. I included some mid-twentieth century pieces, such as the extraordinary chairs upholstered in a hand-painted canvas. For the bedroom, I used a vibrant fabric with drawings of Frida Kahlo and elements related to her art and her culture, such as fruit, flowers, snakes, and pierced hearts. Around the headboard, I placed limited-edition prints from a variety of contemporary artists, including the Kenyan-born Wangechi Mutu. I feel I created a home that my client could identify with, and where she feels grounded and connected to her surroundings.

RIGHT I designed the living room around two mid-twentieth century chairs whose upholstery was hand-painted by an anonymous Brazilian artist. The small glass and bamboo table between the chairs is by the Campana Brothers. Pennsylvania artist Michael C. Begenyi created the abstract geometric acrylic-on-canvas pieces. The standing lamp is from Blu Dot.

OPPOSITE I gathered African dolls from Ghana, South Africa, Tanzania, Kenya, and Nigeria and placed them on top of a set of vintage nesting tables. The colorful fabrics and the beadwork on the dolls' dresses are a beautiful juxtaposition with the canvas behind them.

ABOVE I love how the orange fabric-covered sofas by California designer Edgar Blazona contrast with the cobalt blue of the Moroccan-style rug. I chose different fabrics by Scandinavian designer Josef Frank for the pillows and combined them with a Mexican serape-blanket. On the wall, I hung a series of photographs taken in Mexico by the Seattle-based photographer Paul Souders. The green and orange stools are vintage pieces.

ABOVE Modular shelves from Blu Dot are the focus of one of the walls in the dining area. A group of wood sculptures by Kentucky-based artist L.A. Watson are displayed on one of the top shelves. The striped wallpaper in the adjacent hallway is by the New York-based designer Allison Krongard of Wall Candy Arts. The Orbital standing lamp, by Italian designer Pietro Ferruccio Laviani for Foscarini, is both functional and sculptural.

OPPOSITE The palette of red, yellow, green, and blue in the dining area came from the large acrylic-mounted photograph that I commissioned from South Florida artist Kevin Preston. Vintage vases from Germany were placed on the Chippendale-style credenza. The red powder-coated steel chairs are from Blu Dot. The glass centerpiece on the Pedestal table by Eero Saarinen for Knoll is by Stan O'Neal, an artist who lives in Sedro-Woolley, Washington.

RIGHT I fell in love with this fabric from Alexander Henry, a Burbank, California, company, because it has a lively print of Frida Kahlo. I was so happy that my client liked it and agreed to use it for the headboard in the master bedroom. The white lamps are from Arteriors Home. The collection of limited-edition prints and photographs was chosen from a selection from Artspace.com. Above the bed, *from the left*, is a horse print by the New Orleans-born artist Angelbert Metoyer; a still life by New York-based artist Billy Sullivan; a photograph of a chocolate-covered strawberry by New York artist Sasha Douglas; a collage of a woman's legs wrapped by a serpent by Kenyan-born artist Wangechi Mutu; and a print by the San Francisco-based artist Kara Maria.

Overscale and Super Fashionable

The first time we spoke, I remember my client telling me how she just couldn't put her apartment together. "I can't believe this place looks like my college dorm room!" she said. I told her that that was precisely the reason she had called me. She is a young but very well-respected corporate executive who had lived in London and Tokyo, and when the time came for her to return to her native New York, she chose a tree-lined street in Manhattan's Sutton Place. While the 1,400 square-foot apartment had nice bones, it was a mess. In the beginning, I never thought she was going to let me push so far and so boldly with my design. We began by thinking about how we could make the apartment truly captivating. I knew that we needed to use the mesmerizing English wallpaper I had spotted a while ago when I was in Paris. I could not take my mind away from this bold retro print of dramatic hibiscus in grey and salmon tones. I told my client: "If you want radical changes, this will do it, and we are going big!" As I'm very inspired by fashion, I drew several ideas from the runway for the design of this apartment. Designer Marc Jacobs, in his 2011 Spring/Summer collection, showed glorious Napa leather belts with huge hibiscus, one of which I had to have and wore to the point of almost ruining it. Every time I looked at it, I would see the same flowers as on the wallpaper. I developed the color palette from fashion shows, shopping, and traveling, and decided that the oversized printed flowers were too amazing to ignore. I took a huge risk, but the results were breathtaking.

LEFT I wore a dress by Australian designers Sarah-Jane Clarke and Heidi Middleton, who founded the company Sass & Bide, to the annual Party in the Garden at the Museum of Modern Art in New York in 2012. The dress is made up of different fabrics and textures: The bodice is a weave of linen and silk, and the skirt is sequined all over. Pink suede and glittery silver open-toed booties from Miu Miu completed the outfit. The peach, salmon, and tangerine tones inspired the color palette of this project.

OPPOSITE Dutch artist Ruud van Empel creates sublime photographic compositions, often images of children and nature, which are shot on separate occasions and then masterfully combined. The custom-made Italian mosaic cabinet is from Ercol, a furniture design company in New York.

ABOVE This is how the apartment looked before I redecorated it. Busy young professionals in New York do not have much time to design a single room, much less an entire apartment. My client often told me that the mess was "dragging her down."

LEFT I had all the original black metal window frames in the apartment painted white. The Moorish-style rug is by New York designer Madeline Weinrib, the tangerine armchairs came from CB2, and the pillows on the chesterfield sofa are by New York-based designer Judy Ross. The cabinet above the mantelpiece was custom-made, and the fireplace tools, with their handles in the shape of unicorn heads, are from the 1960s.

OVERLEAF The Arizona wallpaper from British company Osborne & Little makes such an impact that not much else is needed on the walls of this apartment. The hanging fixture is from Restoration Hardware. The dining table was custom-made by From the Source, after my client and I went to their huge warehouse in Brooklyn to choose a slab of wood. We settled on an Indonesian mango that had never been joined or cut in half—the solid piece makes the table all the more special. To counter-balance the drama of the wallpaper, I added a series of Ghost chairs by the French designer Philippe Starck and placed a bamboo centerpiece by the Campana Brothers on the table.

I AM INTRIGUED BY PATTERNS I like the hypnotic effect that repetition brings to the eye, and wallpaper is all about patterns and repetition. Most of the time, I think bolder is better and I'm inclined to choose hyper-saturated prints with enthralling designs. In my own apartment, I have wallpaper in the master and the kids' bedrooms, and I also covered my powder room with a bold red wallpaper in the 1950s *Tema e Variazione* pattern of plates by Italian designer Piero Fornasetti. Almost all of my projects include wallpaper. I believe in its power to change the whole look of a room like nothing else. Lately, I have also experimented with mural-type wallpapers. I'm always looking for new designs and new companies, although classics, like the *Hexagon* wallpaper that English designer David Hicks created in the 1960s, which is now produced by Cole & Son, still do the job in more conservative settings.

LEFT AND BELOW LEFT My client's office area originally included a very messy desk against a wall that contributed to making the whole apartment look like a college dormitory room, which was exactly what she wanted to avoid. I took an underutilized closet and painted it tangerine to harmonize its design and palette with the rest of the public areas. The desk was custom-made, and the shelves are from Ikea. The framed postcards, by British artist Julian Opie, were published by the Alan Cristea Gallery in London. They offer the same lenticular movement as the artist's larger and more important pieces.

OPPOSITE Danish design company Ferm Living's retro leaves are fun and funky; Dallas-based Whimsey Chronicles created these two fanciful patterns, one in blue and coral tones and the other in teal, lilac, and yellow; I love the geometric design composed of triangles also by Ferm Living; Scottish designer Morag Macpherson made this super-cool patchwork wallpaper using all of the fabrics that she had designed in the past; Swedish company Sandberg was inspired by stickers from travels around the world; British house The Art of Wallpaper manufactures subtle yet compelling designs, as seen in this pink paper with abstract motifs; Tres Tintas, a company based in Spain, produces this humorous paper with a cacophony of faces; Albany, a company based in England, makes the colorful brick wallpaper.

RIGHT I'm thrilled that my client went along with my proposal for the bedroom. I chose a very intense apple green for the walls, which contrasted well with the deep cranberry hues of both the vintage Uzbek suzani on the bed and the Moroccan-inspired rug by Madeline Weinrib. The chandelier, a globe comprised of delicate lotus flowers, was handmade of capiz shells. The settee, which I covered in an olive-green velvet, has become one of my client's favorite pieces on which to read.

The vintage Italian Lucite and chrome chandelier adds glamour to the space.

The exposed column shows an interesting architectural detail. The fact that it is round softens an otherwise strong angular element and harmonizes with the rest of the space.

Glass surfaces were important for this space since my client likes to see light reflected everywhere. The see-through dining table accomplishes that without adding visual clutter.

The open shelves under the kitchen counter add another layer of architectural interest that is also functional.

Color Me Different

The loft was sterile and mostly empty when I first went to meet with its owner, an extraordinary marketing genius with one of the best senses of humor I could ever hope for in a client. "This place lacks life" was the first thing he told me. He was right. After many long conversations, I decided to incorporate interesting art, vibrant accessories, chandeliers, cool pieces of furniture, and splashes of color to enliven the place and make it a home, at the same time reflecting my client's unique personality. He is a man who is as much in love with New York as I am. And as the New York lovers that we are, I chose a Brooklyn Bridge piece by Israel-born, New York-based artist Isack Kousnsky to be the central focus of the dining area. The size of the limited-edition digital C-print was customized for my client after I requested that the artist print the image horizontally instead of vertically, as it was originally shown in the movie *Wall Street: Money Never Sleeps*, where I first spotted it. During the time that I was designing this apartment, I watched the movie, where I saw the artwork I knew would make my client happy. In fact, Oliver Stone himself had chosen the piece for the bedroom of the loft that actors Shia LaBeouf and Carey Mulligan shared. Once I saw it, I couldn't pay attention to the characters' dialogue—I was too consumed with trying to figure out who was behind that piece of art! As soon as I left the movie theater, I began my search for the artist who had created such a compelling rendition of the Brooklyn Bridge. It took me a while to find him. When my client and I eventually visited him in his SoHo studio, he fell in love with the image and concurred with my choice. We both still can't believe that it was first seen in that movie!

A large mirror with a red acrylic frame is an additional way to add more color to this room as well as visually amplifying the space and bouncing light back from the windows.

American artist Marilyn Minter's *Green Pink Caviar* video art runs in the living room. It is one of Minter's most provocative films.

The jointed, flexible Artemide floor lamp has been designed to look delicate yet strong.

On the wall behind the dining table, the rendition of the Brooklyn Bridge in red and blue by New York-based artist Isack Kousnsky is contemporary and very close to my client's heart. An emotional connection with art means everything.

Judy Ross makes the best hand-embroidered pillows in the most interesting color combinations. Here, the interlaced ovals keep the eye engaged.

THESE PAGES The open kitchen and combination living-and-dining area, so common in New York, was transformed from a very sterile space. I put up wallpaper in the kitchen instead of the traditional tile backsplash. I was lucky to find a few rolls of this vintage paper with a pattern of the *Wall Street Journal*, sprayed with graffiti'ed letters—so cool and so New York. The limited-edition Andy Warhol skateboard is a fun detail that keeps the eye entertained and always has guests talking. The red pillows on the sofa are by Judy Ross. The stainless steel bowl on the dining table is by the Campana Brothers. The 1950s Lucite and steel chandelier is Italian.

TOP Although I'm not a fan of television sets in living rooms, I often have to negotiate with my clients. Here, as a compromise, I bought *Green Pink Caviar,* a video by artist Marilyn Minter, from the Salon 94 Gallery, which complements the apartment's decor when no one is watching sports or movies. The blue chair was modeled after classic 1950s Scandinavian lounge chairs. The coffee table is by the American designer Warren Platner for Knoll. The abstract sculpture is by Alex Liebau, a New York artist.

ABOVE The Nicolas Pichon mixed media-on-wood panel is from Envie d'art in Paris.

TOP The master bedroom is moody and sexy, with charcoal walls and a lush shag rug. The custom-made red leather chair brings a punch of color that adds character without being overpowering. The diptych above the custom-made dark wood bed is by German artist Jens Nagel.

ABOVE The office and guest room became a very cozy space to hang out in. The oil-on-canvas on the wall is by New York-based abstract neo-expressionist Hunt Slonem; the ottomans are vintage and reupholstered in brown velvet; and the Sputnik lamp on the side table is a flea-market find.

Primary Palette

The client, a very talented, multifaceted, and smart musician, started off with a blank slate. The location of the loft in the West Village, near the Hudson River and all the fun shops and restaurants on Bleecker Street, was irresistible to the client when he decided to buy the space. When I visited the apartment for the first time, I loved seeing guitars, keyboards, and ukuleles all over the place and ready for an impromptu gig. But in reality, it was an empty loft bursting with possibilities. One of the coolest features of my design was the idea of developing a palette of primary colors—red, yellow, and blue—for the living room. A few months before designing this apartment, I had spent the summer in Barcelona and was really taken by that outstanding city. Barcelona is an important cultural center for art and design— one of the facts that makes Catalans boast that they are from the same place where Joan Miró was born. Miró used mostly red, yellow, and blue in his art. His museum, the Fundació Joan Miró, which he founded and built on top of the mountain of Montjuïc, which overlooks the entire city of Barcelona, offers the largest collection of Mirós in the world. My trip to Barcelona got me deeply interested in primary colors. I also spent hours looking at books with works by Fernand Léger, Piet Mondrian, Alexander Calder, and Pablo Picasso, all of whom had either experimented with or

devoted long periods of their careers to working with this classic combination of colors. I wanted to somehow take references from this important modern art period and mix it with cutting-edge contemporary art. I found an interesting Mondrian-inspired wallpaper that I decided to use for the open kitchen. The wallpaper doesn't take itself too seriously and becomes a focal point that anchors the long combination living-and dining rooms. I also went to Patrick McNeil and Patrick Miller, the outstanding men who form the Brooklyn-based street-art duo FAILE, and asked them to put together an installation of prints and one-of-a-kind works. I was inspired by the multihued personality of my client and felt that I could continue designing in a lighthearted way, using colors liberally in the office, and being more moody and subdued in the master bedroom. Aside from the FAILE installation, I selected contemporary art pieces, taking into consideration my client's experiences, tastes, and inclinations. In the end, we were both thrilled with the outcome.

OPPOSITE The vivid prints were chosen specifically for my client and the space by FAILE. As is usual in their art, FAILE plays with subtle references to sex and eroticism. The pharmacy lamp and mirrored table, both vintage pieces, are French.

ABOVE Red, one of my favorite colors, stands out against the neutral background of the open space. The sofa is by the furniture design company Gus Modern, the large red pillows are by the New York-based ThomasPaul, and the Middle-East–inspired ones are from Jules Pansu, a French company. The glass and chrome coffee table is Italian. The primary-colored balancing blocks, from The Future Perfect, were designed by Fort Standard, a Brooklyn-based studio. To soften the design of the molded metal Mars chairs, I added a Moroccan ottoman. The chairs, by the Hong Kong-based designer Timothy Oulton, were reupholstered in vintage distressed leather. The gorgeous rug by ThomasPaul proved to be a perfect anchor for the living room area. The red ottomans were custom-made. I added a stenciled-rendition of a girl on a swing modeled after the works of the anonymous street artist known as Banksy on the wall across from the kitchen. It keeps the playful energy within the context of street art, which is what I wanted when creating the collection for the apartment.

PREVIOUS PAGES I love how everything comes together in the palette of blue, red, and yellow Barcelona-inspired, modernism-influenced tones. The skylight brings an extraordinary amount of light to the space that now feels happy and vibrant. The dining table was created by Timothy Oulton out of reclaimed wood from old boats, and the mid-century modern chairs, designed by Danish designer Niels Otto Møller, were reupholstered in a canary-yellow fabric. The large piece above the piano is by the San Francisco-based artist David Hewitt, whose mixed-media work incorporates urban references and objects found on the street.

LEFT The antique table was an heirloom from my client's grandmother. I paired it with a tall, contemporary acrylic column by Chris Cook, an Indiana-based artist. The vases, which I found in New York's Chinatown, complement the piece in a really interesting way, bringing a series of curved shapes to a vignette with primarily straight lines.

OPPOSITE ABOVE The vintage wood console, probably from an old pharmacy, was turned into a perfect storage solution.

OPPOSITE Vintage decanters from Paris were placed on top of the piano to make a pert statement.

OVERLEAF The wallpaper in the kitchen that was inspired by the geometric works of Dutch painter Piet Mondrian caught my eye when I saw it on a trip to London many years ago. The red pendant lamps and the barstools tie the scheme together. I found the blue and white Greek china at ABC Carpet & Home in New York.

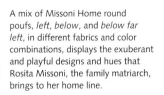

The magic of Capellini in collaboration with the young Swedish designers of Glimpt Studio brings this gorgeous grouping of stools called "Superheroes," developed with skilled sea-grass weavers in Vietnam. The patterns were designed by Swedish illustrator Malin Koort.

A mix of Missoni Home round poufs, *left, below,* and *below far left,* in different fabrics and color combinations, displays the exuberant and playful designs and hues that Rosita Missoni, the family matriarch, brings to her home line.

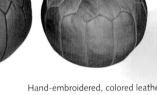

Hand-embroidered, colored leather Moroccan poufs are some of the most versatile ethnic pieces, and can be incorporated into almost any space.

I love Scottish-born designer Donna Wilson's textiles. Her gorgeous knitted fabrics are made of thin lamb's wool, adorned with original, playful designs. In New York, the shop The Future Perfect carries her wonderful creations, including these poufs.

The brilliant Latex Roll Pouf by the Italian design trio 13 Ricrea was created by "upcycling" waste material discarded by the Italian shoe industry.

OPPOSITE A mid-twentieth-century–style chandelier became the focal piece in the home office that also doubles as a guest room. The New York collage mural wallpaper is by Mr Perswall, a Swedish company. I ordered a custom-made red leather Chesterfield sofa and paired it with a colorful pouf and pillows by Donna Wilson. The yellow floor lamps are by the New York designer Robert Sonneman, and the red office chair, which was inspired by the Golden Gate Bridge in San Francisco, is by the Swiss designer Yves Behar for Herman Miller. The modular carpeting is from FLOR.

These ottomans, produced by Hay Studio, a design collective in Denmark, are made with antique Indian saris and are each one-of-a-kind.

OPPOSITE The artwork of a girl on a swing, which was modeled after the graffiti painted by the artist known as Banksy, has a relaxed, stylized look as well as a certain degree of mystery.

ABOVE For this sexy and atmospheric bedroom, I combined the dark charcoal color of the walls with red and yellow accents. The bed was custom-made, with a headboard of camel-colored leather. The nightstands are from Blu Dot. The hand-knotted rug, with its pattern of peacock feathers, was loomed by Indian artisans. The two artworks on the wall are by the consummate New York artists: Romare Bearden, on the left, and Francesco Clemente, on the right.

Brazilian Bossa Nova

A Brazilian couple who are busy professionals, and their two young children, made New York their home several years ago when they purchased a spacious apartment on the Upper East Side. A few pieces of mid-twentieth–century furniture made the living and dining rooms look neat, but quite spare. They had no accessories or art, the kitchen was old and outdated, and the bedrooms were almost empty. Since I'm familiar with the culture of Brazil, I knew that making my clients happy would require a dose of contemporary art from that country. In addition, when I saw the bare foyer, I immediately felt that we could take advantage of its ample size and create something special that would "wow" anyone who came in the door. I was inspired by Brazilian landscape architect Roberto Burle Marx's design of the sinuous 1970s sidewalk that lines Ipanema, Rio de Janeiro's sexiest beach. I'm so glad my clients liked the idea, as the result is breathtaking. The bright colors and excitement in the living room were created with accessories such as embroidered throw pillows, red ottomans, and stools in interesting materials and shapes. The Vik Muniz diptych is the true *pièce de résistance*. I showed my clients several other options by the artist, but we all fell for the impact of *The Creation of Adam, After Michelangelo* from the series *Pictures of Junk*. For the dining room, I bought a large collection of vintage hand-blown glass decanters and bottles to place on the credenza. My clients were also open to buying artwork by other international artists, some not necessarily Brazilian, so I was

happy to introduce them to the work of the German artist Hans Kotter, who creates light boxes, light columns, and LED sculptures. The one I placed in a corner of the living room was developed by Kotter after looking at the colors of an oil drop through light. Its rhythm, intense hues, and movement are absolutely mesmerizing. The American-born and Amsterdam-based painter Nina Bovasso, the French artist Fabrice Thomas, and the abstractionist painter Grant Wiggins are also included in the collection. Wallpaper was important, as the foyer, the kitchen, the master bedroom, the girl's bedroom, and the playroom all have different types of wall-coverings that range from grass cloth to Swedish murals to British classics. Since my clients wanted their home to feel international, every space has furniture, art, and accessories from all over the world. This project represents the melting pot that is New York. I'm thrilled to have captured it!

OPPOSITE The floors were modeled after landscape architect Roberto Brule Marx's Ipanema sidewalk, *above left*. I had artist Christopher Pearson work his magic with several coats of oil-based paint and layer upon layer of polyurethane.

LEFT In the kitchen, I had the cabinets lacquered in a high-gloss white paint and updated the hardware. I also put up a stunning wallpaper of Moorish tiles by Stefan Hengst, a photographer who enlarges images from his travels in Andalucía, Spain. The molded plastic chairs by Charles Eames are very adaptable.

OPPOSITE The mahogany built-ins became more interesting when filled with family photographs in different frames, and books that were relevant to my clients' lives.

OPPOSITE BELOW The remarkable 2011 diptych by Vik Muniz, entitled *The Creation of Adam, After Michelangelo,* was perfect for the space, as the size of both pieces together allowed for maximum impact, and the colors helped bring the room together while keeping the eye engaged. It is from the Muniz *Pictures of Junk* series, in which he arranges garbage found in landfills and on the streets of Brazil to echo iconic artworks and masterpieces. In this piece, he replicated Michelangelo's famous *The Creation of Adam*, the fresco in the Sistine Chapel in the Vatican.

RIGHT A cotton throw by Creativando, an Italian company, and a pillow decorated with a drawing by Pablo Picasso, by the French company Jules Pansu, make graphic statements on the Eames lounge chair. The Hans Kotter light sculpture in the corner is simply stunning.

TOP The dining room looked fantastic after Priscila De Carvalho, a talented Brazilian artist, installed her large mixed-media artwork and its fiberglass cloud extensions on the wall. The collection of vintage bottles that I assembled included ones from France, Poland, the Czech Republic, the United States, Hungary, and Italy. The centerpiece on the Knoll Pedestal dining table by Eero Saarinen is by Italian designer Gaetano Pesce for Fish Design.

ABOVE I convinced De Carvalho to personally install her piece, *Parachutes II*, which includes a custom-made set of fantastic tangerine and royal blue clouds that are applied directly to the wall. This installation was really a treat, and a fantastic opportunity to see an artist in action, choosing the exact spots on which to place each of her pieces.

OPPOSITE Another corner of the dining room offers a view of a magnificent canvas by New York City-based artist Nina Bovasso, called *Beckoning Giacometti*. It complements a side table by Warren Platner for Knoll and a pair of mid-twentieth–century chairs with woven seats.

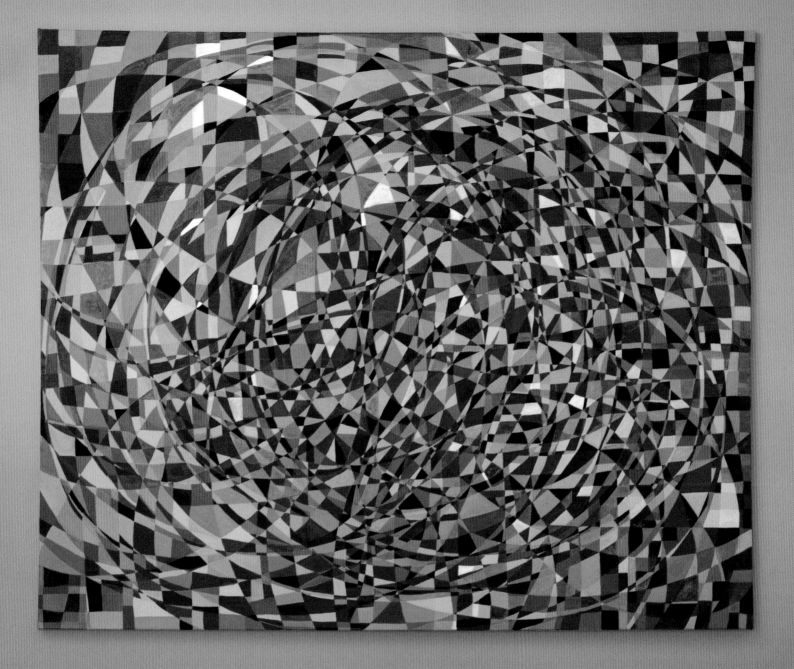

OPPOSITE FAR LEFT The girls' bedroom was inspired by a fabulous patchwork wallpaper made by Paper Moon, a British company. I decided to counterbalance the addiction to pink with a light aqua color.

OPPOSITE An old rocking chair was reupholstered with an Otomi fabric that I purchased directly from Mexican Indians, whose amazing hand-embroidered textiles are pieces of art. The mixed-media wood panel on the wall is by Fabrice Thomas, a French artist. I spotted it in Paris when I visited Cathy Bombard at the gallery Envie d'art and immediately called my clients to say they had to have it.

OPPOSITE BELOW FAR LEFT The boy's room was conceived around a combination palette of green, blue, and yellow. I used a psychedelic fabric from the 1970s to reupholster a Womb Chair by Eero Saarinen for Knoll. I designed bedding for the crib, mixing and matching a variety of differently patterned fabrics. The storage container that resembles Lego blocks is from Bad Apple, a New York-based company. The hanging balloons by the Dutch company Authentic Models are whimsical and come with rattan baskets, hand-knotted netting, sandbags, and a flag.

OPPOSITE Since New York is an international city, I wanted to create a multi-cultural and accepting environment in the playroom. The map of the world and the wallpaper with flags is by Mr Perswall, a Swedish company. The flag pillows are by British designer Timothy Oulton.

RIGHT To reinforce New York's melting-pot culture, I designed shadow boxes with baroque frames filled with rag dolls from all over the world.

OPPOSITE In the master bedroom, I placed a superb dresser made of wood and a patchwork of silk pieces from the Name Design Studio in Istanbul. The vintage chair was lacquered in white and reupholstered in a hot-pink chenille. The small print is by the Japanese artist, Yoshitomo Nara.

ABOVE While the bedroom feels peaceful, a good amount of color keeps it from looking bland. The chevron-patterned wallpaper is by Sanderson, an English firm. The bedside tables are from Oggetti, a store in the Design District of Miami, Florida. The rug is by Thomas Paul, and the throw is from Baobab, a boutique in Paris. The four prints above the bed are by the Arizona-based artist Grant Wiggins.

Fearless Pop

This high-ceilinged loft is special and airy, and
has the feeling of the authentic old-school
hardscrabble industrial spaces of downtown
New York. The architectural elements and the
hardwood floors provide warmth, while the
renovated open kitchen gives the space a more
contemporary look. When I design, I often mix
and match furniture, details, and accessories
from different styles and periods, adding pieces
of contemporary art to reflect the personalities
of my clients. The expansive layout allowed
me to install a few interesting large-scale
pieces. I selected them from a variety of works
and media by different artists, which share an
effervescent *joie de vivre*. The vivid pop colors
in the art pieces create an arresting and fluid
dialogue. When developing an art collection,
the pieces displayed together in the same
room should talk to each other, if not always
harmoniously, at least in a neighborly way.
The wallpaper, a collage of black-and-white
vintage photographs and newspaper
advertisements, Renaissance women with
intriguing expressions, and dramatic red roses,
came from Sweden. Like foyers and powder
rooms, hallways present an opportunity to use
daring elements that could be considered too
much in other rooms: Since we don't spend
too much time there, when my clients allow
me to, I like to add a surprising and bold
element to these spaces. The wallpaper in this
hallway is truly one of a kind. When my client
saw what I had chosen, I got a resounding
"Wow!" and "Yes!"

RIGHT People often forget to decorate
hallways, but I believe that they're a great
opportunity to be wild and crazy, since they
are transitional spaces and nobody spends
too much time there anyway. So why not be
bold? In this hallway, the wallpaper rocks
the house! Made by the Swedish company
Mr Perswall, it has the coolest mix of vintage
and contemporary design. At the end of the
hallway, I placed a baroque mirror lacquered
in red above a small striped console.

OVERLEAF The open configuration of the loft
allows for angles where all of the art can be
seen from any corner of the room. The Andy
Warhol-inspired work of Marilyn Monroe
above the L-shaped sofa is by George Boulter,
a Swiss artist. The vintage credenza came from
Milwaukee, and the mixed media-on-wood
panel above it is by the French artist who goes
by the name of Joseph and who is represented
by the Envie d'art Gallery in Paris. Decidedly
Pop Art-inspired, it creates a harmony with the
other pieces that I had selected. I played around
with plates from Whitbread Wilkinson on the
custom-made zebra-wood table.

LEFT The red suede-upholstered late-1960s easy vintage chairs have been paired with original Ikat pillows from Turkey. The mirrored table is a French antique.

BELOW LEFT The vintage console is a piece of art. With a combination of wood and brass plates, it was reinvented by an artisan in Milwaukee who used an embossing treatment and then painted the doors and drawers with an antique brass paint that was oxidized to achieve a blue-green patina.

OPPOSITE In the dining area, the American flag has been rethought by German artist Freddy Reitz. With embedded words and references to New York City, it is bright and eye-popping. The artisanal mango-wood bowl and tray are from Indonesia.

Housing Works

I was thrilled to be invited by Mel Alvarez from Housing Works' *Design on a Dime* event to participate in what has been called New York's most popular interior design benefit. Along with about 50 terrific designers, I was asked to create a room or vignette with merchandise that has been donated to the charity and sold to the attendees for 50 to 70 percent off its retail price. The profits from sales are invested in housing projects for homeless and low-income New Yorkers living with and affected by HIV/AIDS. Housing Works is an amazing charity that has been doing exceptional work since 1990. For my vignette, I envisioned something really colorful with contemporary art, of course, that my clients would not let me do for them. I wanted an amalgam of unique elements and was delighted that all the people I reached out to wanted to help. My great friend Craig Appelbaum, the owner of the Industry Gallery in Washington, D.C., and Los Angeles, donated an aluminum rocking chair by Israeli artist Shlomo Assaf Harush. It's called *Crushed Can*, and became the *pièce de résistance* that everyone touched, wanted to sit down on, and buy. I covered the walls of my space in an Italian vintage wallpaper from the 1970s that I bought at Vintage Galaxy, a store in Messina on the island of Sicily, Italy. Its owner has been obsessed with retro patterns from the 1970s and 1980s since he was a little boy, and he spends his life renovating houses in Sicily, teaching guitar students old and new tunes, and always looking for rolls of original antique and vintage wallpaper. I chose a fuchsia wallpaper with Egyptian-inspired motifs in yellow, lilac, and light brown. By the time we installed it, I was mesmerized by it and so was everyone who stopped by. It was a magical wallpaper. But the booth would have been incomplete without a good selection of art. I was lucky to get Eli Sudbrack from AVAF, the Suzanne Geiss Company in New York, and Artspace.com on board. Sudbrack graciously donated an installation of five AVAF pieces that were strategically placed to contrast with the wallpaper. When the huge number of editors, writers, designers, and celebrities came into the Metropolitan Pavilion on opening night, the first thing that flew off the walls were those five limited-edition prints.

RIGHT My *Design on a Dime* booth represented aspects of who I am as a person and as a designer. Mixing the old with the new, I certainly did not shy away from contemporary art, wallpaper, and extreme colors. Besides the fabulous wallpaper, the rocking chair, and the prints by AVAF, I added a rug from a N.Y. Conran Shop and pillows made with Scandinavian fabrics. The powder-coated steel red chair, another favorite, is from Blu Dot.

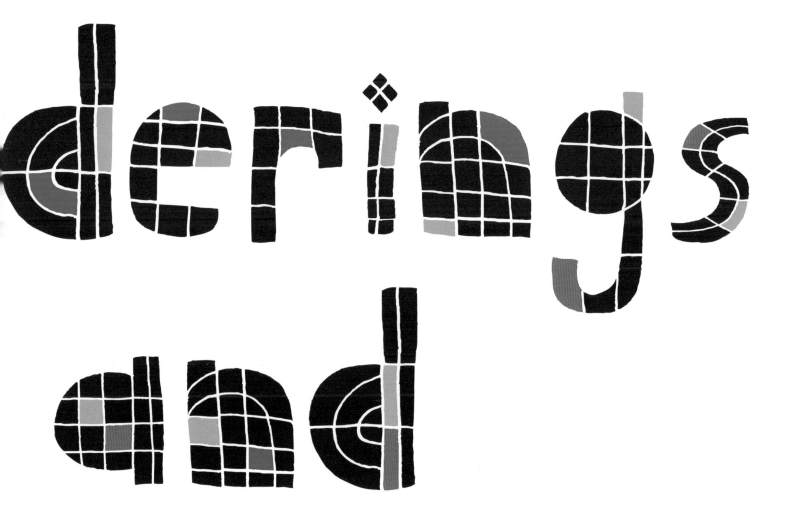

derings and
er

PLACES I LOVE

Traveling is one of my passions. All of my travels have influenced my work, in one way or another. There isn't a place that I have visited where I have not brought clothes, jewelry, or decorating accessories back with me. Every one of my projects has an accessory, an entire wall, or a rug that has been influenced by one of my excursions around the world. Traveling turns ordinary objects into conversational pieces with a history, a culture, and a story to tell. Traveling keeps me curious, hungry, and open-minded. However, no place in the world has inspired me as much as the city that I have been calling home for the past 12 years. My New York represents the beautiful, the bad, and the ugly, a roller coaster of ups and downs, mean streets, sweet triumphs, boisterous failures, a resiliency of the spirit, the materialization of the impossible, high fashion, unorthodox style, an overpowering energy, the center of contemporary art, the irrepressible, and the irreverent. New York has been so generous to me and is still ripe with opportunity. It is poetic and dramatic, romantic, and prosaic, intense, and all-consuming. And yet, everything makes so much sense to me. The outpouring of creativity that I get simply from walking down the streets of Manhattan can give me enough fuel to create wild designs, even if I weren't feeling inspired before. It's no coincidence that poets, artists, filmmakers, writers, actors, musicians, as well as many other creative personalities have fallen for New York. I am not an exception. Paris is another city that has inspired me enormously. I am always fascinated by the purity of the light, the people walking leisurely and enjoying their surroundings, the carefully edited and selective boutiques, the many squares and parks, the markets, the appreciation for handmade and artisanal objects, the obsession with craftsmanship, beauty, haute couture, and Oh, the Champagne, *aussi*. Paris is a city driven by very contemporary design, if not in architecture, then in its concentration of the best design and furniture shops and galleries in the world. I haven't made a trip to Paris where I have not spent at least one day walking happily in the pursuit of new discoveries, which is, in my opinion, the best way to wander the cobblestoned streets of the City of Lights. Barcelona has rocked my world with its wild combination of some of the best buildings in the world, by such architects as Antoni Gaudí, Ludwig Mies van der Rohe, and Santiago Calatrava, which happily coexist with a mix of Catalan modernism, baroque, gothic, and contemporary design. This is in a seaside city that has it all: beaches, museums, shops, galleries, and *mucha marcha*. The city is a paradise for foodies, as even the dishes served in the hundreds of restaurants are arranged artistically to please the sharpest of eyes and palates. Barcelona being such a walkable city, one can spend hours in a maze of tiny streets in the *Barrio Gotico, El Born,* and even the grittier *El Raval*—all of which are full of curious stores, charming cafés, and chic boutiques. Cape Town in South Africa and Rio de Janeiro in Brazil share a very similar landscape of curvy beaches bordered by sexy sidewalks. They are large cities built next to the ocean and exuberant mountains that seem to keep an eye on the frenetic pace of the urban metropolis that lies below. Even the lifestyles of these two cities, which are so remote from each other, are similarly

filled with bikinis, flip-flops, beautiful bohemian people, colorful street fairs, and gorgeous beaches that delight tourists and natives alike. The vibrant ethnic fabrics from South Africa, along with beaded dolls, embroidered linens, and woven baskets have remained in my heart and in the back of my mind for many years. Italy is full of treasures—from North to South and coast to coast. Rome is mysterious and legendary, and feels so much like a Pandora's Box—I never really know what I am going to find next. The impeccable style that Romans flaunt, regardless of the season, and their fearless color permutations are really a feast for the eyes. The Amalfi Coast, with its contrasting scenery of Mediterranean blues, bougainvillea, lime trees, bright and colorful tiles, and mellow houses in carmine, ochre, coral, and crimson that seem painted using a *trompe l'œil* technique, have kept me dreaming ever since I first went there. As for Greece and Turkey: Both are quite mystical, very seductive, and have their own personality. Greece has the most sensuous islands, like Santorini, Hydra, and Mykonos, with striking white houses that seem almost pasted against the intense blue patches of ocean. Turkey has huge cities, like Istanbul and Ankara, both of which are abundant in bazaars and flea markets bursting with textiles, lamps, leather goods, spices, caftans, tunics, pottery, and perfumes, all of which make me almost delirious, engaging all my five senses at the same time.

LEFT, FROM TOP In the summer of 2011, Oliver and I enjoyed El Barrio Gotico in Barcelona; I went shopping in Le Marais neighborhood in Paris on a cold day in the spring of 2010; and in Barcelona, I posed in an installation by the Japanese-born artist Yoshi Sislay.

OPPOSITE I was 12 weeks pregnant with my younger son, Oliver, when this picture of Daniel and me was taken in Pérouges, a charming medieval village in the Rhône-Alpes region of France. It's impossible not to be touched by the beauty of the wall-enclosed town, where there is something new waiting to be discovered around every corner. I was wearing a limited-edition dress by Diane von Furstenberg, which she designed using Andy Warhol prints.

OVERLEAF I could not do my job without having the possibility of travel around the world in such places as France, South Africa, Spain, and the Mediterranean islands. New York, however, is the lifeblood of my designs and the center of my creative process.

Chinatown T-shirts

Galeries Lafayette cupola

Vintage map of Manhattan

At the Palais Royal

Soho buildings

Model boats, Jardin des Tuileries

Skyline

Pol Bury sculpture, Palais Royal

Me in Central Park

Café terrace

John Lennon memorial

Flowering balconies

Dinner in Union Square

View from Montmartre

Casa Batlló, Barcelona, Spain

Mykonos, Greece

Ipanema, Rio de Janeiro, Brazil

Positano, Italy

Oliver and me, Lisbon, Portugal

Portofino, Italy

On the Italian Riviera

The Amalfi Coast, Italy

Cape Town crafts, South Africa

Le Sirenuse Hotel, Positano, Italy

Santorini sunset, Greece

Katikies Hotel, Santorini, Greece

Candies, Barcelona, Spain

Sorrentine Peninsula, Italy

AROUND THE WORLD IN 80 SHOPS

In Baobab, in Paris

New York is a paradise for shoppers. There are so many stores in Manhattan and Brooklyn that it's impossible to list all the places where I have found objects, furniture, or clothes, or have simply admired the displays. New York is such an amazing city for shopping that I have been in such remote places as Cape Town or Bora-Bora and have found a piece that I had to have, only to return to Manhattan to find a similar one in a store that I hadn't noticed before. Shopping in New York confirms the saying: "If you can't find it in the Big Apple, it doesn't exist." The shopping experience becomes even more dynamic when I travel around the world shopping for myself or my clients. I have been in situations where my husband is driving down an unknown road in a foreign country and I ask him to stop—most of the time, against his will—because I spotted a store that I needed to explore. Once when I was in Southampton, New York, I saw two gorgeous mid-twentieth–century chairs upholstered in an unusual fabric in the window of a shop that I did not remember from the previous summer. I told my husband to stop, ran in, and bought the chairs on the spot for one of my clients, and even negotiated a discount. I was back in the car in exactly seven minutes. Design, good taste, visual merchandising, and originality have no nationality or price point. I have found extraordinary accessories and furniture in run-down or hole-in-the-wall places, as well as in high-end retailers. I do not disregard any sources, as I believe that playing the game of scavenger hunt is one of the most exciting parts of what I do. Time and time again I find myself back in shops that stay on my radar forever because they provide a level of service and innovation, whatever the merchandise may be. When I go shopping, I get ideas, I touch fabrics, I talk to salespeople, I connect with others, I hear stories, I dream. In New York, I love **ABC Carpet & Home** which was opened more than 100 years ago by the Weinrib family. Nowadays, they have two buildings: The original one is devoted to the core business of rugs of all kinds, from contemporary plush carpets to 150-year-old Turkish kilims, and the newer one operates as a department store, with hundreds of brands and edited selections that range from the English **Conran Shop** in the basement, to **Kartell**, the Italian emperors of high-end plastic design. There are also colorful ethnic pillows, throws, poufs, and accessories and furnishings from Indonesia, South Africa, India, Thailand, and many more exotic places around the world. I also get excited every time I go to **The Future Perfect** on Great Jones Street. The selection of objects, lighting, and furniture is always ahead of the curve. The store represents luminaries of the design world, such as Dutch furniture designer Piet Hein Eek and the British textile and product designer, Donna Wilson. I have never gone into The Future Perfect and left empty-handed. On the Bowery, right across from the New Museum, **Artware Editions** has a very extensive collection of both functional and purely decorative objects, wallpaper, and furniture made in collaboration with contemporary artists. The store's limited-edition set of Limoges china with artist Cindy Sherman's self-portraits as Madame de Pompadour in Limoges is mind-blowing! I sometimes go to **Patricia Field**'s store, also on the Bowery, to jumpstart my creativity and to think outside the box. Field is a fantastic stylist who has been working with celebrities, television, and film producers for years. She is a born and bred New Yorker, and the consummate stylist for *Sex & the City*. Everything in the store is either hand-picked or designed by her, and she continually adds art and accessories. Sometimes, her jewelry and accessories are so over the top that I have to ask myself: Would Carrie Bradshaw wear this?

Close by, **Dashwood Books** is entirely devoted to photography books, including some rare or out-of-print editions, special collaborations, and collectibles. Concept fashion stores, such as **Jeffrey** in the Meatpacking District and **Kirna Zabête** in SoHo, provide countless hours of inspiration. The owners of Kirna Zabête, Beth Buccini and Sarah Easley, are so attuned to the fashion world and everything that is stylish and chic—from shoes to accessories to jewelry to books—that for more than ten years, they have consistently turned trends into classics, spotted the big, new talents, and presented avant-garde designs from the haute-couture runway shows as well as by unknown recent graduates from the Parsons School of Design. I know that if they pick a new designer to be a part of their exclusive selection, there's quite a chance that he or she will become a rising star in the fashion world. I go to Kirna Zabête to get ideas from the colors, patterns, materials, and structural cuts and combinations, as all of these clues get translated into my projects in one way or another. Kirna Zabête is located on what I call SoHo's Design Row, on Greene Street, where some of my favorite design stores include: **Moroso**, an Italian store with the most amazing pieces of furniture, fabrics, and objects; **Artemide,** with its world-class lighting and fixtures; **Alessi**, with its cool and contemporary home accessories; **Taschen Books**, where an amazing mural by Brazillian artist Beatriz Milhazes covers the walls; **B&B Italia,** the company that manufacturers some of the best sofas and lounge chairs in the world; and **Design Within Reach,** which has recreated and revived many mid-twentieth–century pieces that were almost impossible to find a few years ago. **Ingo Maurer**, who designs lamps that look like magical sculptures, is on the corner of Greene and Grand streets, and the **Isabel Marant** boutique, on the corner of Broome Street, which was designed by French architect Nicolas André and looks like an art gallery with high ceilings, raw wood racks, and an unmistakable industrial-glam vibe. Parallel to Greene Street, Wooster Street also has a number of design stores that I can't help but run into: **Poltrona Frau,** which remains faithful to its origins in Turin, Italy, and is committed to quality; **Cappellini**, another Italian wonder that produced, among many other drool-worthy pieces, a modern chair upholstered in Pucci fabric; **Eclectiques,** with its extraordinary selection of antique and vintage pieces; **Blu Dot**, a newcomer from Minnesota, whose furniture designs quickly won me over; **Dune**, with its ingenious and colorful furniture; **Property**, which has a spectacular selection of contemporary furniture and accessories from hundreds of chic, mostly European, designers; **The Rug Company,** the English emporium that produces rugs that are pieces of art by fashion designers, artists, and many other creative people; and the **Phaidon Bookstore.** On West Broadway, **Treasure & Bond** is a store in an 11,000-square-foot industrial space that has a great selection of both known and virtually unknown designers, artists, and jewelry-makers. All of their profits benefit children's charities in New York. **Sobral**, also on West Broadway, is the brainchild of Brazilian designer Carlos Sobral. The store carries the most fantastic jewelry and objects for the home made of plastic resin in the most intense colors I have ever seen. **R 20th Century**, a beautiful space that operates both as a gallery and as a store, is further West on Franklin Street, in TriBeCa. It has a large selection of pieces by modern designers that ranges from the famous Danish furniture designer Verner Panton to the Brazillian Campana Brothers. In New York's West Village, I am always tempted to buy something at **Bookmarc** because what could be sexier

Fundació Joan Miró

Barcelona

Fundacio Joan Miró

Loja CCB in Lisbon

The Future Perfect

Nap Atelier

Vinçon

Ivo & Co.

Miu Miu

Evil eyes in Greece

I always say I have the best job in the world because I get to shop for my clients in the most beautiful stores in New York and anywhere else I have the opportunity to travel to, such as Paris, Barcelona, or Cape Town.

Funky necklaces in Istanbul

10 Corso Como

The Galleria in Milan

African beaded crafts

Textiles in Provence

Olde Good Things

than fashion designer Marc Jacob's bookstore? This tiny spot on Bleecker Street carries a very well-curated selection of new, vintage, and rare books on art, design, fashion, film, and architecture. **The End of History** is a gorgeous place filled with colorful hand-blown vintage glass pieces, bottles, decanters, lamps, and hanging fixtures from Italy, Germany, Sweden, and the Czech Republic. **Adelaide** is very glamorous and carries formidable furniture and accessories from the 1930s to the 1960s, with an emphasis on Art Deco pieces. In the East Village, **White Trash** on E. Fifth Street is a well-kept secret for mid-twentieth–century and vintage pieces. The prices alone are worth the visit, though the merchandise rotates quite often and most things fly off the shelf very quickly. Also in the East Village, **Lobel Modern** is a super-selective store, gallery, and showroom, with pieces from the 1940s to the 1980s, mostly by American designers, displayed in a luxurious setting. I'm also a fan of the **John Derian Company** and **John Derian Dry Goods** because the coasters, plates, trays, and other découpage-inspired things are such fun. The myriad Moroccan rugs are also fantastic, as are the ethnic textiles and sets of bed linens. **La Sirena**, also in the East Village, is a tiny store that has all sorts of Mexican handicrafts, textiles, and folk items that I like to mix and match with more contemporary pieces for an unexpected look. In Chelsea, my neighborhood, there are also lots of incredible shops: **Authentiques Past and Present** has a wonderful selection of vintage glass, antique games, and lamps from the 1950s and 1960s; **Coolhouse** has some of the best and, as its name implies, coolest and most arty small pieces of furniture, carefully selected by its owner; **Les Toiles du Soleil** is a piece of the South of France in New York, with a bright and happy selection of striped fabrics, pillows, and acrylic trays; the **Showplace Antique + Design Center** is a great space with a variety of dealers mostly of Art Nouveau, Art Deco and mid-twentieth–century furniture and objects. Some of the dealers also have vintage clothing, jewelry, and accessories; **Maison 140** is beautifully stocked with European, mostly French, products; **Mantiques Modern** is a place like no other, with literally thousands of vintage objects, sculptures, leather trunks, Pop Art and Op Art pieces, and collections of random objects that when displayed make perfect sense together; **Olde Good Things** has a vast selection of architectural details, from marble mantels that came from the Plaza Hotel, to antique French carved-wood doors and antique furniture and mirrors; **Story** is an amazing concept store whose focus changes every four to six weeks, almost like a magazine, and which presents different collections around a specific theme—love, color, and New York are recent topics. Although all over the city and the United States, my favorite **Anthropologie,** which has successfully channeled the hippy-chic, gypsy-bohemian style, is the one in the Chelsea Market. I love their trinkets, ceramics, vases, and glasses, but it is their fantastic collection of upholstered settees, sofas, and lounge chairs that takes first prize. Finally, **192 Books,** next to the Clement Clarke Moore Park, has the best art and design books in a small, beautiful space, which also presents art exhibitions. When in Midtown,

I've often spent hours at the **MoMA Design and Book Store,** which is not only impressive in size but is also on the main floor of my favorite museum in the whole world—as well as in a large space across the street. On the Upper East Side, the design shop at **Phillips de Pury** on Park Avenue has books, artists' editions and multiples, and one-of-a-kind objects. **Barneys New York,** whose ninth floor I love to wander through, always carries the ultimate statement pieces, pillows, throws, and accessories. **Maison 24** on East 64th street has brought sexy back to the Upper East Side, with colorful and graphic objects as well as furniture, games, lots of acrylic Lucite and neon. **Doris Leslie Blau** is a rug showroom where almost everything is unusual, special, and a stand-out that has been hand-picked by its owner. **Buck House** has a very cool, edited, and artfully displayed selection of vintage pieces, accessories, rugs, and china from all over the world. **Eileen Lane Antiques** offers lots of amazing Art Deco and mid-twentieth–century pieces.

PARIS FAVORITES:
Colette, which pretty much started the concept store frenzy, still carries the best of the best in fashion and unique designs. **Arty Dandy** is fabulously creative and offers fashion, art, and unusual objects, and almost everything has an undeniable sense of humor. **Sentou** has some of the coolest designs for the home, and carries great stuff for kids, especially the 100drine collection. **Merci** is located in an enormous airy space that feels quiet and zen, while at the same time presenting fashion, accessories, kitchen items, and a selection of ethnic furniture and upholstered pieces that is exceptionally good. **La Galerie Moderne** has many pieces by such great Italian architects as Gaetano Pesce and the late Ettore Sottsass, Jr. **Electrorama** has an impressive selection of lamps from the 1960s to today. **La Boutique Scandinave** carries plenty of Scandinavian designers, both known and soon-to-be-known. **Steiner** represents hard to find designers like Kwok Hoi Chan, whose chromatique modules I love. **Caravane** captures the bohemian chic style so well, as does **Baobab,** with its colorful vintage patchwork fabrics, pillows, and throws. **107 Rivoli,** in the shopping arcade under the Musée des Arts Décoratifs, has innovative tableware, costume jewelry, and an interior design and architecture bookstore like no other in Paris. **Printemps Design,** the shop at the Centre Georges Pompidou, is also full of inspirational design objects. **Serendipity** offers one-of-a-kind pieces and exclusive collaborations with designers from around the world. I also love everything at department store **Le Bon Marché,** whose clothing selections are really edited to show the best brands and the most exclusive pieces. The second floor, which was re-named the Maison d'Edition, has more than 80,000 square feet of the absolute best of fine living, including furniture by Charlotte Perriand and Jean Prouvé, Vitra pieces, David Weeks lamps, hundreds of unique stationery sets, and a bookstore with some of the best design, art, fashion, and architecture books.

BARCELONA FAVORITES:
I love **Vinçon,** the mecca of style and design, with its rows and rows of objects, toys, dinnerware, furniture, and more. **Ivo & Co,** the fantastic retro-vintage shop in the El Born neighborhood, has an offshoot across the street exclusively dedicated to kids' furniture, textiles, accessories, and objects. **La Comercial** has five stores of fashion and home décor. **Papeles Pintados Aribau** carries thousands of wallpapers, many of them produced exclusively for this beautiful store. **L'Appartement** showcases the work of young Spanish designers. **The Original Cha Chá** has several collections of tableware items, tea sets, and funky objects designed in partnership with Spanish designers, such as Agatha Ruiz de la Prada and Alexis Rom.

MILAN AND GENOA FAVORITES:
10 Corso Como is one of the most beautiful stores in the world and includes the most imaginative displays, a fantastic terrace and café, a gallery, and even three hotel suites! My other favorite, which is so different from 10 Corso Como, is **Nap Atelier,** where the attention to detail, small production, and one-of-a-kind pieces make me dream about designing beautiful furniture one day. **Via Garibaldi 12** is a home design store that is so impressively beautiful, it's worth the trip to Genoa. Marble checkerboard floors, infinitely high ceilings, a palatial structure, gilded walls, and an outstanding selection of furniture from contemporary designers and artists such as Richard Woods of British-based design company Established & Sons, as well as crystal from Baccarat and Venini.

LISBON FAVORITES:
In Bairro Alto, **Gezo Marques,** a designer whose workshop is open for visits, has created some of the most stunning pieces with vintage and antique woods in different shapes, colors, and sizes. **Oficina à Lapa** is another shop that designs and manufactures incredible objects, lamps, and accessories, all with that mix of cool contemporary and vintage elements that Lisbon does so well.

CAPE TOWN FAVORITES:
Africa Nova is a spectacular store that imprints African originality and craft onto contemporary designs. **Merchants on Long** is set up in an historical building erected by the Dutch in the mid-1800s and carries textiles, jewelry, pillows, toys, and clothing, all with an African-chic touch. **T & Co** is part safari-chic and part Cape-Dutch style, with a selection ranging from large pieces of furniture to fabrics. The colorful Africa Café tableware of **Clementina van der Walt Ceramics** typifies the expansive beauty of South Africa.

MADRID FAVORITES:
Close to the famous El Rastro, **Antigüedades Las Nuevas Galerías** is a 1940s building with a huge courtyard in the middle that encompasses more than 60 shops selling antiques and vintage pieces from all over the world. I can easily spend hours browsing there. **Gastón y Daniela,** with its numerous locations in the city, has beautiful upholstery fabrics and textiles, as well as a new line of wallpapers. **Isolée** is a concept store that is a little bit overwhelming because it has so much: fashion, beauty, books, home decorating items, and food. I always find something here that I have never seen anywhere else before.

For addresses and websites, see page 152.

ABOVE Patricia Field on the Bowery in New York is filled with apparel, jewelry, and home accessories.

RIGHT Via Garibaldi 12 is a concept store located in an over-the-top-palazzo built in 1562, only a 45-minute drive from Portofino on the Italian Riviera, and about an hour and a half from Milan. Inside, genius pieces of contemporary furniture, unique china, textiles, and vases share the space with baroque stucco decorations and frescoes that depict scenes from the Punic War.

INSPIRED BY HOTELS

For me, traveling is synonymous with great experiences and wonderful hotels. When I happen to not be traveling a lot, I often frequent the hotels in New York to get inspired, bypassing an international commute. Hotels are usually designed to wow people and to pamper their guests. And who doesn't want to be wowed and pampered for a few days? I am particularly influenced by hotels that have a very decisive and strong vibe—sexy, romantic, fun, or artsy. Good hotels focus on details and, as a designer, details mean everything to me—from the right soap in the powder room, to the bottle of Champagne in the fridge, to the freshly ironed bed linens. I have put together a list of some of my favorite hotels. It was not easy to make a short selection because I have traveled and seen so many. **The Ritz** in Paris: I can't think of a more romantic place in a more romantic city. The Ritz, which opened in 1898, is iconic in every way. Some people say that it's too touristy, too busy, and that the Place Vendôme is noisy. Oh God, they don't know what they are missing! The Ritz is the Parisian hotel that has the largest ratio of staff to guests, and the service is impeccable. Its history is as rich as the combination of baroque and rococo furniture and carpets. So many interesting guests have made The Ritz their home, including Coco Chanel, who lived there for more than 30 years, and Ernest Hemingway, who sparked the creation of the hotel's fabulous Hemingway Bar. One of the things I love the most about The Ritz is its willingness to remain true to itself without sacrificing comfort and service. That is what I strive for with my clients and my designs. The amber fragrance that impregnates the lobby, hallways, and rooms, is so compelling that I bought several bottles from the gift shop and spray them in my home when I want to be reminded of the hotel. I never ignore the power of home fragrance: It makes any place so much more personal and can trigger strong and happy memories time and time again. **Le Sirenuse** in Positano: European hotels are not always huge or overly luxurious, but they can be incredibly special. Le Sirenuse is one of those gems that has been owned and managed by the Sersale family for the past 60 years. Perched at the top of the Positano hills above the Amalfi Coast in Italy, Le Sirenuse is the closest I have felt to being in a real family home while staying in a hotel. Every room is completely different from each other, except for the fact that each one has a magical view. There are fragrant lemons, limes, and oranges everywhere, and every time I think of Le Sirenuse, I put fruit in my home as well as in my clients'. The typical Italian tiles of the Amalfi Coast on the floors and the furniture were chosen by the Sersales. Like good Italians, they are unafraid of bright greens, blues, and yellows. The building itself is painted in an intense shade of carmine red. The linens are from Frette. After spending a week at Le Sirenuse, the first thing I did when I came back to New York was to change all my sheets to Frette linens. Sometimes it just takes little things, like having high-quality bed linens, to feel good, happy, and pampered in your own bed. **Katikies** in Santorini: This little hotel in the Cyclades is like an island within an island. Everywhere you look, your eyes focus on the intense

Outside the Ritz in Paris

At the Katikies in Santorini

shades of the infinite blue Aegean Sea. All the free-form architecture, which defines Santorini as a whole, is as white as can be. The amazing contrast of white and blue has stuck with me ever since. The experience at Katikies is breathtaking—the hotel charms you and makes you fall in love with it. It is impossible to forget. When we were there, I was pregnant with my first son and remember having a super-enhanced sensitivity to colors, smells, and sights. I could not have been more impressed by this simple yet dramatically beautiful hotel. I always try, in one way or the other, to add some blue and white to my designs. It's my homage to Santorini and the Katikies. **The Hotel on Rivington**: Sexy, sexy, New York sexy. Since my birthday is in January—which is the dead of winter and also when work is in full steam—we usually don't go anywhere to celebrate. My husband Marcio, however, once surprised me with a whole package of activities for my birthday weekend, part of which was spending the night at the Hotel on Rivington. I was thrilled. The views from the Lower East Side are so different from what New Yorkers are typically used to seeing in midtown or uptown. Our suite had almost 360-degree views of the city. I'm not a minimalist, but the Rivington is a perfect example of a place that doesn't need curtains because the views say it all. **60 Thompson**: Hotels for drinks? Absolutely! Hotels are always a fun place to meet and hang out for lunch, dinner, or cocktails at the end of the day. I love lobbies bursting with interesting-looking people wearing crazy outfits. And I love 60 Thompson for being chic but also simple, for flawlessly executing the concept of the boutique hotel in such a huge city. I love the terrace, the bar, and Kittichai, their Thai restaurant, which has been a favorite of mine for years.

The Gramercy Park Hotel: American artist Julian Schnabel designed this hotel lobby, its acclaimed bar, and curated its first art collection. Since then, the hotel has rotated the most amazing art, and every time I go there for a drink at the Rose Bar or the Gramercy Terrace, I'm bedazzled by the pieces on the wall, which range from Andy Warhol to Damien Hirst, and everything in between. There is also a lot of rustic wood to balance the strength of the art and make the place feel warm. The colors are strong and beautiful. It's the matador red, the Prussian blue, and the Spanish Flamenco influence that make this place feel unique and full of energy.

For more of my favorite hotels, see page 153.

OVERLEAF On a recent trip to the Italian Riviera, we visited the Hotel Splendido in Portofino, where I was photographed on one of its terraces. The Splendido is one of the most celebrated places in the world, not only because of its extraordinary and impeccable service, but also because of its sumptuous setting, magnificent surroundings, lush gardens, and unparalleled views of the Portofino Bay.

The Ritz in Paris

Soho House in New York

Le Sirenuse Hotel in Positano

Hôtel Costes in Paris

Katikies in Santorini

Le Sirenuse Hotel in Positano

The Delano in Miami Beach

Maybe it's because I work so hard when I'm in New York that I am drawn to staying at lavish hotels when I travel. Certain design elements from each of these hotels leave me so inspired that I often call on aspects of them in my own designs.

Hotel Splendido in Portofino

The Hotel on Rivington in New York

The Gramercy Park Hotel in New York

Singita Lebombo in South Africa

Gild Hall in New York

Casa Fuster in Barcelona

MARIA'S GO-TO GUIDE

GALLERIES
NEW YORK
Danziger Gallery
527 West 23rd Street
New York, NY 10011
(212) 629-6778
www.danzigerprojects.com

Eleven Rivington
11 Rivington Street
New York, NY 10002
(212) 982-1930
www.elevenrivington.com

Gladstone Gallery
515 West 24th Street
New York, NY 10011
(212) 206-9300
www.gladstonegallery.com

James Cohan
533 West 26th Street
New York, NY 10001
(212) 714-9500
www.jamescohan.com

Lehmann Maupin Gallery
540 West 26th Street
New York, NY 10001
(212) 255-2923

201 Chrystie Street
New York, NY 10002
(212) 254-0054
www.lehmannmaupin.com

Lumas Gallery
362 West Broadway
New York, NY 10013
(212) 219-9497
www.lumas.com

Paul Kasmin Gallery
293 10th Avenue
New York, NY 10001

515 West 27th Street
New York, NY 10001
(212) 563-4474
www.paulkasmingallery.com

Praxis Art
541 West 25th Street
New York, NY 10001
(212) 772-9478
www.praxis-art.com

Salon 94
12 East 94th Street
New York, NY 10128
(646) 672-9212

243 Bowery
New York, NY 10002
(212) 979-0001

1 Freeman Alley
New York, NY 10002
(212) 529-7400
www.salon94.com

Sikkema Jenkins & Company
530 West 22nd Street
New York, NY 10011
(212) 929-2262
www.sikkemajenkinsco.com

The Hole
312 Bowery
New York, NY 10012
(212) 466-1100
www.theholenyc.com

WASHINGTON, D.C.
Industry Gallery
H St./Atlas Historic District
1358 Florida Avenue, NE
Washington, DC 20002
(202) 399-1730
www.industrygallerydc.com

PARIS
Galerie 208
208 boulevard Saint Germain
75007 Paris, France
+33 01 42 50 30 24
www.galerie208.fr

Galerie Envie d'art
4 Avenue Bugeaud
75016 Paris, France
+33 01 55 73 10 76

29 Boulevard Raspail
75007 Paris, France
+33 01 42 84 40 29

24 Rue Treilhard
75008 Paris, France
+33 01 53 30 00 10
www.enviedart.com

Galerie Eva Hober
35-37 Rue Chapon
75003 Paris, France
+33 01 48 04 78 68
www.evahober.com

Galerie Kreo
31 Rue Dauphine
75006 Paris, France
+33 01 53 10 23 00
www.galeriekreo.fr

Galerie Perrotin
76 Rue de Turenne
75003 Paris, France
+33 01 42 16 79 79
www.perrotin.com

School Gallery
81 Rue du Temple
75003 Paris, France
+33 01 42 71 78 20
www.schoolgallery.fr

LONDON
Lazarides Gallery
8 Greek Street
London W1D 4DG, UK
+44 (0)20 3214 0055
www.lazinc.com

Paradise Row
74 Newman Street
London W1T 3DB, UK
+44 (0)20 7636 9355
www.paradiserow.com

Victoria Miro
16 Wharf Road
London N1 7RW, UK
+44 (0)20 7336 8109
www.victoria-miro.com

White Cube
48 Hoxton Square
London N1 6PB, UK
+44 (0)20 7930 5373

144-152 Bermondsey Street
London SE1 3TQ, UK
+44 (0)20 7930 5373

25-26 Mason's Yard
London SW1Y 6BU, UK
+44 (0)20 7930 5373
www.whitecube.com

AROUND THE WORLD
Gagosian
980 Madison Avenue
New York, NY 10075
(212) 744-2313

555 West 24th Street
New York, NY 10011
(212) 741-1111

522 West 21st Street
New York, NY 10011
(212) 741-1717

456 North Camden Drive
Beverly Hills, CA 90210
(310) 271-9400

7938 Ivanhoe Avenue
La Jolla, CA 92037
(858) 458-9428

6-24 Britannia Street
London WC1X 9JD
+44 (0)20 7841 9960

17-19 Davies Street
London W1K 3DE
+44 (0)20 7493 3020

4 Rue de Ponthieu
75008 Paris
+33 01 75 00 05 92

800 Avenue de l'Europe
93350 Paris, Le Bourget
+33 01 48 16 16 47

Via Francesco Crispi 16
00187 Rome
+39 06 4208 6498

3 Merlin Street
Athens 10671
+30 210 36 40 215

19 Place de Longemalle
1204 Geneva
+41 22 319 36 19

7/F Pedder Building
12 Pedder Street
Central, Hong Kong
+852 2151 0555

STORES
NEW YORK
192 Books
190 10th Avenue
New York, NY 10011
(212) 255-4022
www.192books.com

ABC Carpet & Home
888 & 881 Broadway
New York, NY 10003
(212) 473-3000
www.abchome.com

Adelaide
702 Greenwich Street
New York, NY 10014
(212) 627-0508
www.adelaideny.com

Alessi
130 Greene Street
New York, NY 10012
(212) 941-7300
www.alessi.com

Anthropologie
75 9th Avenue
New York, NY 10011
(212) 620-3116
www.anthropologie.com

Artemide
146 Greene Street
New York, NY 10012
(212) 334-7222
www.artemide.us

Artware Editions
270 Bowery
New York, NY 10012
(212) 463-7490
www.artwareeditions.com

Authentiques Past and Present
255 West 18th Street
New York, NY 10011
(212) 675-2179
www.fab-stuff.com

B&B Italia
138 Greene Street
New York, NY 10012
(212) 966-3514
www.bebitalia.it

Barneys New York
660 Madison Ave
New York, NY 10065
(212) 826-8900
www.barneys.com

Blu Dot
140 Wooster Street
New York, NY 10012
(212) 780-9058
www.bludot.com

Bookmarc
400 Bleecker Street
New York, NY 10014
(212) 620-4021
www.marcjacobs.com

Buck House
1318 Madison Avenue
New York, NY 10128
(212) 828-3123
www.buckhouse.com

Cappellini
152 Wooster Street
New York, NY 10012
(212) 620-7953
www.cappellini.it

Coolhouse
211 West 19th Street,
New York, NY 10011
(212) 254-4790
www.coolhouseantiques.com

Dashwood Books
33 Bond Street
New York, NY 10012
(212) 387-8520
www.dashwoodbooks.com

Design Within Reach
110 Greene Street
New York, NY 10012
(212) 475-0001
www.dwr.com

Doris Leslie Blau
306 E. 61st Street
New York, NY 10065
(212) 586-5511
www.dorisleslieblau.com

Dune
156 Wooster Street
New York, NY 10012
(212) 925-6171
www.dune-ny.com

Eclectiques
483 Broome Street
New York, NY 10013
(212) 966-0650

Eileen Lane Antiques
236 East 60th Street
New York, NY 10022
(212) 317-1289
www.eileenlaneantiques.com

The End of History
548 1/2 Hudson Street # A
New York, NY 10014
(212) 647-7598
http://theendofhistoryshop.
blogspot.com

The Future Perfect
55 Great Jones Street
New York, NY 10012
(212) 473-2500
www.thefutureperfect.com

Ingo Maurer
89 Grand Street
New York, NY 10013
(212) 965-8817
www.ingomaurer.com

Isabel Marant
469 Broome Street
New York, NY 10013
(212) 219-2284
www.isabelmarant.com

Jeffrey
449 West 14th Street
New York, NY 10014
(212) 206-1272
www.jeffreynewyork.com

John Derian Company
6 East 2nd Street
New York, NY 10003
(212) 677-3917
www.johnderian.com

John Derian Dry Goods
10 East 2nd Street
New York, NY 10003
(212) 677-3917
www.johnderian.com

Kirna Zabête
96 Greene Street
New York, NY 10012
(212) 941-9656
www.kirnazabete.com

La Sirena
27 East 3rd Street
New York, NY 10003
(212) 780-9113
www.lasirenanyc.com

Les Toiles du Soleil
261 West 19th Street
New York, NY 10011
(212) 229-4730
www.lestoilesdusoleilnyc.com

Lobel Modern
39 Bond St #1
New York, NY 10012
(212) 242-9075
www.lobelmodern.com

Maison 24
470 Park Avenue
New York, NY 10022
(212) 355-2414
www.maison24.com

Maison 140
140 9t Avenue
New York, NY 10011
(212) 255-0022
www.maison140nyc.com

Mantiques Modern
146 West 22nd Street #1
New York, NY 10011
(212) 206-1494
www.mantiquesmodern.com

MARIA'S GO-TO GUIDE

MoMA Design and Book Store
44 West 53rd Street
New York, NY 10019
(212) 708-9400
www.moma.org

Moroso
146 Greene Street
New York, NY 10012
(212) 334-7222
www.morosousa.com

Olde Good Things
124 West 24th Street
New York, NY 10011
(212) 989-8401
www.ogstore.com

Patricia Field
306 Bowery
New York, NY 10012
(212) 966-4066
www.patriciafield.com

The Phaidon Bookstore
83 Wooster Street
New York, NY 10012
(212) 925-1900
www.phaidon.com

Phillips de Pury
450 Park Ave #1
New York, NY 10022
(646) 588-7680
www.phillipsdepury.com

Poltrona Frau
145 Wooster Street
New York, NY 10012
(212) 777-7592
www.frauusa.com

Property
14 Wooster Street
New York, NY 10012
(917) 237-0123
www.propertyfurniture.com

The Rug Company
88 Wooster Street
New York, NY 10012
(212) 274-0444
www.therugcompany.com

R 20th Century
82 Franklin Street
New York, NY 10013
(212) 343-7979
www.r20thcentury.com

**Showplace Antique +
Design Center**
40 West 25th Street
New York, NY 10010
(212) 633-6063
www.nyshowplace.com

Sobral
412 West Broadway
New York, NY 10012
(212) 226-2710
www.sobralusa.com

Story
144 18th Street
New York, NY 10011
(212) 242-4853
http://www.thisisstory.com

Taschen Books
107 Greene Street
New York, NY 10012
(212) 226-2212
www.taschen.com

Treasure & Bond
350 W Broadway
New York, NY 10013
(646) 669-9049
www.treasureandbond.com

White Trash
304 East 5th Street
New York, NY 10003
(212) 598-5956
www.whitetrashnyc.com

PARIS
107 Rivoli
107 Rue de Rivoli
75001 Paris, France
+33 1 42 60 64 94
www.lesartsdecoratifs.fr

Arty Dandy
1 Rue de Furstenberg
75006 Paris, France
+33 1 43 54 00 36
www.artydandy.com

Baobab
18 Rue Saint Croix
de la Bretonnerie
75004 Paris, France
www.baobab-home.fr

Caravane
6, rue Pavée
75004 Paris, France
+ 33 1 44 61 04 20
www.caravane.fr

Colette
213 Rue Saint-Honoré
75001 Paris, France
+33 1 55 35 33 90
www.colette.fr

Electrorama
11 Boulevard Saint-Germain
75005 Paris, France
+33 1 40 46 78 11
www.electrorama.fr

La Boutique Scandinave
8 Rue Martel
75010 Paris, France
+33 1 40 22 02 67
www.laboutiquescandinave.com

La Galerie Moderne
52 Rue Mazarine
75006 Paris, France
+33 1 46 33 13 59
www.lagaleriemoderne.com

Le Bon Marché
24 Rue de Sèvres
75007 Paris, France
+33 1 44 39 80 00
www.lebonmarche.com

Merci
111 Boulevard Beaumarchais
75003 Paris, France
+33 1 42 77 00 33
www.merci-merci.com

Printemps Design
Place Georges Pompidou
121 Rue Saint Martin
75004 Paris, France
+33 1 44 78 15 78
www.printemps.com

Sentou
26 Boulevard Raspail
75007 Paris, France
+33 1 45 49 00 05

29 Rue François Miron
75004 Paris, France
+33 1 42 78 50 60
www.sentou.fr

Serendipity
81 Rue du Cherche-Midi
75006 Paris, France
+33 1 40 46 01 15
www.serendipity.fr

Steiner
80 Boulevard Sebastopol
75002 Paris, France
+33 1 42 72 82 82

67 Boulevard Raspail
75006 Paris, France
+33 1 45 48 94 61

37 Rue du Commerce
75015 Paris, France
+33 1 45 75 29 98
www.steiner-paris.com

BARCELONA
L'Appartement
Carrer d'Enric Granados, 44
08008 Barcelona, Spain
+34 93 452 29 04
www.lappartement.es

Aribau Papeles Pintados
Aribau Street, 71
08036 Barcelona, Spain
+34 93 453 22 58
www.papelespintadosaribau.com

Ivo & Co.
Carrer Rec 20 Baixos 2A
08003 Barcelona, Spain
+34 93 268 33 31
www.ivoandco.com

La Comercial
C/ Bonaire, 4
08003 Barcelona, Spain
+34 93 295 46 30
www.lacomercial.info

The Original Cha Chá
Oliana 8
08006 Barcelona, Spain
+34 93 209 16 41
www.cha-cha.es

Vinçon
Passeig de Gracia, 96
08008 Barcelona, Spain
+34 93 215 60 50
www.vincon.com

MILAN
10 Corso Como
Corso Como, 10
20154 Milan, Italy
+39 02 29002674
www.10corsocomo.com

Nap Atelier
A Viale Piave 19
20129 Milan, Italy
+39 02 796861
www.napatelier.com

GENOA
Via Garibaldi 12
Via Garibaldi 12/1
16124 Genoa, Italy
+39 010 25 30 365
www.viagaribaldi12.com

LISBON
Gezo Marques
Rua João Pereira da Rosa, 8,
1200-236 Lisbon, Portugal
+35 1 91 290 86 55

Oficina à Lapa
Rua Saraiva de Carvalho, 90
1250-244 Lisbon, Portugal
+35 1 213 978 203
www.oficinalapa.pt

CAPETOWN
Africa Nova
Cape Quarter
72 Waterkant Street, Green Point
Cape Town 8001, South Africa
+27 21 425 5123
www.africanova.co.za

Clementina van der Walt Ceramics
Shop c101/b
The Old Biscuit Mill
375 Albert Road, Woodstock
Cape Town 7915, South Africa
+27 21 447 1398
www.clementina.co.za

Merchants on Long
34 Long Street
Cape Town 8001, South Africa
+27 21 422 2828
www.merchantsonlong.com

T & Co
Unit 78 Victoria Junction
Ebenezer Road, Green Point
Cape Town 8005, South Africa
+27 87 808 7064/5

MADRID
Antigüedades Las Nuevas Galerías
Ribera de Curtidores, 12
28005 Madrid, Spain
www.antiguedadesnuevasgalerias.com

Gastón y Daniela
Calle de Velázquez, 42
28001 Madrid, Spain
+34 914 352 421
www.gastonydaniela.com

Isolée
Calle de las Infantas, 19
28004 Madrid, Spain
www.isolee.com

HOTELS
60 Thompson
60 Thompson Street
New York, NY 10012
(212) 431-0400
www.thompsonhotels.com

The Gramercy Park Hotel
2 Lexington Ave.
New York, NY 10010
(212) 920-3300
www.gramercyparkhotel.com

The Hotel on Rivington
107 Rivington Street
New York, New York 10002
(212) 475-2600
www.hotelonrivington.com

Hôtel Ritz Paris
15 Place Vendôme
75001 Paris, France
+33 1 43 16 30 30
www.ritzparis.com

Katikies Hotel
Oia (Ia), Santorini 84702
Cyclades Islands, Greece
+30 22 86 07 14 01
www.katikieshotelsantorini.com

Le Sirenuse
Via Cristoforo Colombo, 30
84017 Positano SA, Italy
+39 89 87 50 66
www.sirenuse.it

ALSO TOP ON MY LIST:
The Auberge du Soleil
180 Rutherford Hill Road
Rutherford, California
(707) 963-1211
www.aubergedusoleil.com

Bora Bora Pearl Beach Resort & Spa
Motu Tevairoa
+68 9 50 84 45
www.spmhotels.com

Cape Grace
130 Victoria Wharf Street
Quay Four
Cape Town 8001, South Africa
+27 21 410 7100
www.capegrace.com

Château de Bagnols
69620 Bagnols
France
+33 4 74 71 40 00
www.chateaudebagnols.com

The Crosby Hotel
79 Crosby Street
New York, NY 10012
(212) 226-6400
www.firmdalehotels.com

The Delano Hotel
1685 Collins Avenue
Miami Beach, FL 33139
(305) 672-2000
www.delano-hotel.com

Four Seasons Hotel Ritz
Rua Rodrigo da Fonseca, 88
1099-039 Lisbon, Portugal
351 (21) 381-1400
www.fourseasons.com/lisbon

Gild Hall
15 Gold Street
New York, NY 10038
(212) 232-7700
www.thompsonhotels.com

The Greenwich Hotel
377 Greenwich Street
New York, NY 10013
(212) 941-8900
www.thegreenwichhotel.com

Hotel Casa Fuster
Passeig de Gràcia, 132
08008 Barcelona, Spain
+34 958 21 59 69
www.hotelescenter.es

Hotel Costes
239 Rue Saint-Honoré
75001 Paris, France
+33 1 42 44 50 00
www.hotelcostes.com

Hotel du Cap Eden Roc
Boulevard John F. Kennedy
06601 Antibes, France
+33 04 93 61 39 01
www.hotel-du-cap-eden-roc.com

Hotel Splendido
Salita Baratta 16
16034 Portofino (GE), Italy
+39 01 85 267 801
www.hotelsplendido.com

The Mandarin Oriental
Passeig de Gràcia, 38-40
08007 Barcelona, Spain
+34 93 151 88 88
www.mandarinoriental.com/barcelona

Singita Lebombo
Malilangwe Wildlife Reserve
Kruger Park, South Africa
+27 (0)21 683 3424
www.singita.com

MARIA'S GO-TO GUIDE

1. Deitch, Jeffrey and Julia Gruen. *Keith Haring*. New York: Rizzoli, 2008.

2. Foix, Vicente and Pedro Almodóvar. *The Pedro Almodóvar Archives*. New York: Taschen, 2012.

3. Friedman, Vanessa. *Emilio Pucci*. New York: Taschen, 2010.

4. Gautrand, Jean-Claude. *Paris: Portrait of a City*. New York: Taschen, 2012.

5. Murphy, Robert and Ivan Terestchenko. *The Private World of Yves Saint Laurent and Pierre Bergé*. New York: The Vendôme Press, 2009.

6. Oldham, Todd and Kiera Coffee. *Alexander Girard*. California: Ammo Books, 2011.

7. Paas, Stephanie. *100 Interiors Around the World*. New York: Taschen, 2012.

8. Passebon, Pierre. *Jacques Grange: Interiors*. Paris: Flammarion, 2009.

9. Tannenbaum, Allan. *New York in the 70s*. New York: The Overlook Press, 2011.

10. Testino, Mario. *Mario de Janeiro Testino*. New York: Taschen, 2009.

WEBSITES

I love shopping on the internet as much as I love the brick-and-mortar experience. Here is a selection of my favorite websites, either to browse, to shop, or simply to be inspired by.

ART

Artnet.com: The most comprehensive art database, Artnet gathers auction results, gallery information, artists' financial performances, graphics pertaining to the art market, and much more.

Artspace.com: This is my favorite online seller of contemporary art. With a click of the mouse, I can order a set of Kara Walker prints or a one-of-a-kind painting by Stephen Westfall. The site also curates and produces its own editions and forges partnerships with galleries, foundations, and museums around the world. The strong editorial content is a plus.

Art.sy: A genius website that characterizes and connects various works of art. Based on an initial artwork search, the website shows collectors and non-collectors alike other works of art that they might like, by artists that they might not have known

or considered before. I love its content, and the galleries that the site has partnered with are some of the best in the world.

LittleCollector.com: Chrissy Crawford had an amazing idea: Why not let kids start their own contemporary art collections? She partnered with artists, museums, and foundations to make this happen, and the prints and editions are gorgeous, fun, and very affordable.

Paddle8.com: With great editorial content and videos, this site builds alliances with museums and lets the world see a museums outstanding pieces, and the overall energy of a show. Paddle8 has also partnered with galleries and art fairs so that, in real time, it allows website members to buy a piece that may be exhibited, for example, at the NADA Art Fair in Miami, even though the collector may be in Moscow at the time.

Phillipsdepury.com: The online catalogs alone are worth the visit. Phillips de Pury is an auction house that has reinvented the concept of the traditional formal auction. With unique themes—such as "BRIC," for Brazilian, Indian, Russian, and Chinese art; and the "80s," comprised mostly of New York-based artists who reached their peak in that decade—created for educational purposes, and an understanding of auction-level prices, Phillipsdepury.com has a lot to offer to both the uninitiated and the experts.

PurePhoto.com: This is a site for lovers of photography, or people looking for inspiration. PurePhoto sells fine photographs by young and seasoned photographers, and also has a social media component for photography addicts who can form groups, follow their favorite people, become friends, and give reviews.

RockPaperPhoto.com: With sexy photographs of the Rolling Stones, an entire series of black-and-white images of Lady Gaga's early days in the East Village, and Axel Rose rocking out on stage, RockPaperPhotos amasses a huge selection of fine photography of music stars, actors, and athletes from all over the world, available for sale to fans and art collectors alike.

SHOPPING

1stdibs.com: Beautifully edited pieces from the fanciest and most respected names in the world of vintage and antique furniture and collectibles, plus gorgeous editorial content in e-magazines that sometimes looks even better than the real thing, make this website a favorite of mine, hands down.

AHALife.com: Every day, Shauna Mei and her team bring a different object, piece of clothing, or accessory to our inboxes. Uniquely curated by a wide group of tastemakers, AHAlife is perfect for those who are looking to discover things not available anywhere else.

eBay.com: Without a doubt, this is one of the most amazing websites ever created. The amount of stuff for sale is really incredible, and the prices are even more so. A simple search can easily yield results that show thousands of items. Buying on eBay can be either overwhelming or incredibly thrilling. For me, it's the latter.

Edition01.com: Jessica Wilpon and Estefania Lacayo created an online playground for fashion designers who want to release limited edition pieces not offered anywhere else. With big names like Proenza Schouler and Vera Wang, Edition01 is the place to go when I want something that no one else is likely to have.

Etsy.com: Artists, artisans, jewelry makers, designers, and the craftiest people from every corner of the planet set up shops on Etsy to surprise and delight with curious finds, ravishing furniture, extraordinary craftsmanship, and reinvented vintage pieces that have been "up-cycled" to look even better than their original forms.

Fab.com: A remarkable flash sale site, Fab has a lot more different categories than others, including designs for kids, accessories for pets, costume jewelry, textiles, prints, clothing, and food.

Kirnazabete.com: If I can't get to the SoHo store in New York, I check out the website, where most of the actual merchandise in the store is also for sale. Since Beth and Sarah are so involved with everything in their shop, I know that what I'm seeing online has been handpicked by them.

Net-a-porter.com: I discovered Net-a-porter when it was only six months old and sold things only in England. I was enthralled by the pieces for sale and the way the outfits were put together. Nowadays, it is the mogul of high fashion sales online, and its editorial features, weekly e-magazines, and videos are drool-worthy. Although sometimes I don't end up buying anything, more often I end up getting a piece of clothing, a pair of shoes, or some costume jewelry. In New York, the site delivers the same day if the order is placed before 2 pm.

OneKingsLane.com: OKL is indeed the King and Queen of home design, furniture, and accessories. The website hosts flash sales, each of which is up for a few days, offering some of the best brands at a fraction of its usual price. I usually want it all.

Thefutureperfect.com: I have already mentioned so many times how obsessed I am with The Future Perfect. The website is almost as good as the shops, as the merchandise selection is large and the description of items is as accurate as it can be.

Vivre.com: Everything on Vivre is curated and carefully selected. The Living and Gifts categories are worth mentioning specifically because they always have unique accessories, art, one-of-a-kind pieces of furniture, china, and glassware that will surprise even the most discerning eye.

RESOURCES AND INSPIRATIONAL CONTENT

Apartmenttherapy.com: Nowadays a classic, this site is a bible of resources, content, and features on real apartments and houses and their interesting owners all over the world.

FreshHome.com: Micle Mihai-Cristian, who lives in Romania, is the head of a team that edits and curates this massive blog daily, with images of the most beautiful interiors around the globe, including never-before-seen pictures of spaces in places as remote as Oslo or Tokyo.

Garancedore.com: Garance is the embodiment of the chic French girl who now calls New York City her home. She's a fantastic illustrator, a wonderful photographer, and a witty writer. I love her stories,

which sometimes are purely about fashion and other times about creative people, places, or anything else that may be tickling her fancy.

Goop.com: Sometimes superstars are truly generous and willing to share all their secrets with the rest of the world. Gwyneth Paltrow's wonderfully edited compilation of favorite places, restaurants, travel guides, shops, recipes, beauty products, and many more valuable resources is presented on Goop in a no-fuss, accessible way.

Marantphiles.com: For my day-to-day activities, I'm usually wearing Isabel Marant, and I must admit that I love looking at editorials of women wearing her designs. The editor, Aliya Armorer, does an amazing job of picking the best to show all of us Marant-obsessed people. On any given day, the "philes" may feature women who are wearing Marant in the streets of Boston or London, or maybe how the latest issue of Korean, Italian, or American *Vogue* styles the highlights of the latest collection.

Mocoloco.com: The latest and most interesting pieces of contemporary furniture design, accents, colors, and art are chosen and presented in a streamlined way by a team of design fanatics who work mostly out of the site's Canadian headquarters. What I like about Mocoloco is that they have really edited their selection, tested products, and actually experienced the products that they endorse and recommend.

Mymarrakesh.com: Maryam Montague and her husband Chris moved to Marrakesh a few years ago, and their architecture and design adventure evolved into a few home renovations, a small hotel, a book, and the precursor of it all: the blog that captures Maryam's Moroccan aesthetic and other north African musings.

Style.com: Style.com shows everything from the latest runway shots, to the pieces that are keeping editors excited, to behind-the-scenes videos and unique collaborations with fashion designers, celebrities, and models. Its resources, addresses, product recommendations, and archives are jam-packed with pictures that leave me browsing for hours.

Theglow.com: Attractive moms and their offspring are photographed in their homes, showcasing beautiful interiors, inspiring ideas and delicious recipes, each with their unique point of view on life and motherhood.

Thesartorialist.com: Ever curious about what the most glamorous people in the world are wearing in Florence, New York, Paris, Madrid or anywhere else Scott Schuman may be shooting? Guess no more and go to The Sartorialist for a great dose of fashion and urban backgrounds that can make nearly everyone daydream for hours.

Theselby.com: Todd Selby photographs and films awesome interiors, with the coolest people from São Paulo, Brazil, to Sydney, Australia, and everywhere else in between. The features he shows are worthy of the glossiest high-end home design magazines.

Trunkarchive.com: As the name suggests, this website is an archive of thousands upon thousands of images from fashion editorials, celebrity features, beauty, and architectural shots from some of the biggest and boldest names in the industry, such as Bruce Weber and Mario Testino.

UnBeige.com: Stephanie Murg writes funny and insightful posts about art, design, architecture, and fashion. I always check UnBeige to read about what's going on in the design world, particularly in New York, where she is based.

INDEX

ACKNOWLEDGMENTS

Thank you:

To Gwyneth Paltrow: This book would not have happened without you or Goop. Your inner and outer beauty and your vast generosity inspire me every day.

To Tracy Anderson: You have taught me that there is no challenge that I cannot tackle. You have infused my day-to-day life with extraordinary drive, persistence, and determination.

To all my grandparents: For always showing me the value of hard work.

To the godparents of my children, Juan Jose, Gabriela, Alex, and Marjorie, for being such extraordinary people.

To Sean Combs, Toni Fletcher, and Sienna Lee: For having given me the wonderful opportunity to work with you.

To Susie Finesman: For connecting the dots.

To Marni Salup: For being such a great cheerleader and an even better publicist. I could not have done it without your energy and enthusiasm.

To Mariette Edwards: For keeping me focused and aligned and always pushing me to become my better self.

To Craig Appelbaum: Who came into my life and has brought only amazing things.

To Suzanne Slesin, my publisher and friend: Thank you for your support and encouragement, for believing in me, and for striking a beautiful balance between being nurturing and passionate and a commander-in-chief.

To Stafford Cliff: I could not have been luckier to have you as my art director. You are the embodiment of the English Gentleman, in every sense of the word.

To Dominick J. Santise, Jr.: For the beautiful visuals in this book.

To the wonderful and dedicated team at Pointed Leaf Press, with whom I have shared so many fun moments: Regan Toews, Deanna Kawitzky, Anita Tan, and Marion D.S. Dreyfus. You guys rock!

To all my clients, who have entrusted me with their homes and art collections. All of you, and your colorful lives, encourage me tremendously. Special thanks to Danielle Campisi, Alan Chapell, Kim Dickstein, Giunero Floro, Patryk and Andrea Merhy, Elena Michaelcheck, and Jordan Taube.

To all the wonderful people in the world of contemporary art: artists, gallerists, curators, and collectors, and especially to Fabiola Beracasa, Cathy and Yann Bombard, Carla Camacho, James Cohan, Corinne Dalle-Ore, Christa Yoo Hyun D'Angelo, Tracey Emin, Kathy Grayson, Julia Gruen, Laurie Harrison, Catherine Levene, Meg Malloy, Patrick McNeil and Patrick Miller, Nick Olney, Gaetano Pesce, Otavio and Gustavo Pandolfo, Ryan Phillips, Nessia Pope, Annelise Ream, Flavia da Rin, Kenny Scharf, Mikhail Sokovikov, Eli Sudbrack, and Jason Aaron Wall.

To all of my friends from all over the world, from New York City to Caracas, London to Barcelona, and everywhere else in between; my TAM friends, my childhood friends, my Harvard friends, and, in particular, those who have supported me and Lifestyling®, followed my adventures, and motivated me with your stories, your lives, and your love.

To the fantastic photographers who, with their magic lenses, have captured the images in this book: Scott Jones, Amalia Mayita Mendez, Scott Gabriel Morris, Jessica Ozment, David Lewis Taylor, and Ellen Warfield.

To Bhano Arbind, for making it possible for me to do my job every day, and for her love, unwavering support, and "always ready" disposition.

To New York, for being my most important muse, and for always being there for me.

Maria Gabriela Brito—November 2012

Photography credits:

Unless noted, all photographs were taken by Ellen Warfield or are personal photographs from the private collection of Maria Gabriela Brito. Any errors or omissions will be corrected in future editions.

11, bottom: Kristy Leibowitz ©The Hole; 12: Illustration by Natali Martinez; 13, center and bottom: David Lewis Taylor [Marilyn Minter]; 14: © CinemaPhoto/CORBIS [Sophia Loren]; S. Bukley / Shutterstock.com [Gwyneth Paltrow]; vipflash / Shutterstock.com [Penelope Cruz]; Lev Radin / Shutterstock.com [DVF]; 15: photo by Guillermo Kahlo © Guillermo Kahlo estate]; 16: Venturelli/ WireImage/Getty Images; 17: Clockwise, from top: © Patrick McMullan.com [Iris Apfel]; Courtesy of KirnaZabete.com [Sarah Easly]; Marcio Souza; Nathalie Lagneau/Catwalking/Getty Images [Isabel Marant]; Jacopo Raule/Getty Images Entertainment/ Getty Images [Dolce & Gabbana with Monica Belucci]; Courtesy of KirnaZabete.com [Beth Buccini]; Marcio Souza; JP Yim/WireImage/Getty Images [Marc Jacobs]; Courtesy of Edition01.com; 18: David Lewis Taylor; 46: Kristy Leibowitz ©The Hole; 47: Courtesy of Industry Gallery; 49: © Beatriz Milhazes / Courtesy James Cohan Gallery, New Y01ork/Shanghai; 50: [inset] Marcio Souza; Art © Vik Muniz / Licensed by VAGA, New York, NY; 51: [inset] Marcio Souza ; 52: [inset] Marcio Souza; Courtesy of Lehmann Maupin and Tracey Emin; 54–55: Courtesy of Flavia Da Rin; 56–57: Courtesy of Christa Joo Hyu D'Angelo; 58: Marcio Souza; 68: [middle] Neale Cousland; 69: Matt Sarraf; 70: [inset] Marcio Souza; Courtesy of Os Gêmeos; 71: Photo by Allen Benedikt Courtesy of Deitch Archive and Os Gêmeos; 74: [Second from top] Jessica Ozment; 78: Scott Jones ; 79: [bottom] Scott Jones ; 80–82: Scott Jones; 84–85: Scott Jones; 86–93: Jessica Ozment; 94: Billy Farrell/BFAnyc.com ; 95–97: Scott Gabriel Morris; [inset] Maria Brito; 98–103: Scott Gabriel Morris; 116: [From top clockwise: Courtesy of Missoni; Courtesy of The Future Perfect; Courtesy of The Future Perfect; Courtesy of Missoni; Courtesy of 13 Ricrea; Courtesy of Capellini]; 120–121: [Insets] Maria Gabriela Brito; 140–141: Marcio Souza; 142: [First column] Amalia Mayita Mendez; Ashley Van Buren; Kristy Leibowitz ©The Hole; [Second column] Marcio Souza; Thomas Birke; [Third column] Marcio Souza; Christos Drazos Photography/Courtesy of Katikies Hotel; [Fourth column] Courtesy of Le Sirenuse; Marcio Souza; Christos Drazos Photography/Courtesy of Katikies Hotel; 147: Courtesy of Via Garibaldi 12; 148: Marcio Souza; 149: Courtesy of Le Sirenuse; Christos Drazos Photography/Courtesy of Katikies Hotel; Daniel Krieger Photography/ Courtesy of The Hotel on Rivington; Courtesy of Gramercy Park Hotel; Courtesy of SoHo House; Courtesy of Thompson Hotels; 150–151: Marcio Souza; Opposite: © The Keith Haring Foundation; Endpapers: Courtesy of Mexican Indigenous Textiles, www.mexicantextiles.com.

Maria Gabriela Brito is a Venezuelan-born, Harvard-educated, New York-based interior designer, tastemaker, and authority on the mixing of contemporary art with home decoration. She has demystified and democratized the act of collecting art through her company, Lifestyling® by Maria Gabriela Brito, and has designed the homes of her clients with the objective of accomplishing artful interiors. She lives in New York City with her husband and two sons. This is her first book.

COVER The remarkable 2011 diptych by Vik Muniz, entitled *The Creation of Adam, After Michelangelo*, was perfect for one of Maria Gabriela Brito's interior design projects, as its size allowed for maximum impact, and the colors helped bring the room together. Photograph by Ellen Warfield.

BACK COVER On a recent trip to the Italian Riviera, Maria Gabriela Brito was photographed on one of the terraces at the Hotel Splendido in Portofino. Photograph by Marcio Souza.

ENDPAPERS The Otomi fabric is from Mexico and was hand-embroidered by the Otomi Indians.

OPPOSITE HALF TITLE PAGE Maria bought the vintage Mexican serape-blanket in Playa del Carmen, Mexico.

OPPOSITE TITLE PAGE Inspired by traditional Mexican and contemporary design, Maria created a table setting on the terrace of her Manhattan apartment building. Photograph by Ellen Warfield.

OPPOSITE This is the same Keith Haring drawing Maria saw in a gritty subway station on Seventh Avenue and 28th street the first time she came to New York in 1983. She never thought that almost thirty years later she would negotiate major Haring pieces for her clients.

Inquiries should be addressed to:
Pointed Leaf Press, LLC.
136 Baxter Street, New York, NY 10013
www.pointedleafpress.com

Pointed Leaf Press is pleased to offer special discounts for our publications. We also create special editions and can provide signed copies upon request. Please contact info@pointedleafpress.com for details.

Printed and bound in Singapore
First edition
10 9 8 7 6 5 4 3 2 1
Library of Congress Control Number: 2012951384
ISBN: 9781938461033